D0207161

Try Tracking!

The Puppy Tracking Primer

Carolyn A. Krause

Dogwise™ Publishing

Wenatchee, Washington U.S.A.

Try Tracking! The Puppy Tracking Primer
Carolyn A. Krause

Dogwise Publishing

A Division of Direct Book Service, Inc.
PO Box 2778
701B Poplar
Wenatchee, Washington 98807
1-509-663-9115, 1-800-776-2665
website: www.dogwisepublishing.com
email: info@dogwisepublshing.com

Graphic Design: Shane Beers — Cincinnati, Ohio
Cover photo Askonandy's Encore in Blue, TD, "Cory" at 10 weeks. Owned by
    Barb Steward. Photos by the author, Lisa Finger and Dogwise Publishing.
Thanks to Ross B. Young for the illustrations "Complete Summer Tracker" and
    "Complete Winter Tracker."
Portions of this book appeared in the self-published booklet "The Puppy Tracking
    Primer" by the author.

Library of Congress Cataloging-in-Publication Data

Krause, Carolyn, 1943-
Try tracking! : the puppy tracking primer / by Carolyn Krause.
    p. cm.
ISBN 1-929242-18-2
ISBN 978-1-929242-18-4
1. Puppies--Training. 2. Tracking dogs--Training. 3. Dogs--Training. I. Title.
SF431.K74 2005
636.7'0887--dc22

                        2005003279

ISBN: 1-929242-18-2   Printed in the U.S.A.
ISBN: 978-1-929242-18-4

Dedication

*This book is dedicated to my dogs and to my husband, Mike, who
have been wonderful partners in all my adventures in dog training.*

A TIP OF MY HAT

Each of us involved in tracking owes a great debt to those who preceded us.
Here is a tip of my hat to all those anywhere who have tracked dogs and
have shared their knowledge with the rest of us. Glen Johnson, who was
the first to develop a "recipe" for training a tracking dog. To John Bernard,
former AKC Field Representative for tracking, who always shared his experi-
ences, wisdom, and thought-provoking ideas with us.

A big thank you to Charlene, Larry, Barb, Lindsay, and Nate at Dog-
wise Publishing. Without their excellent editing and belief that this book
was "a real winner," you would not be reading it now. And to everyone who
has authored a book, pamphlet, or article on tracking training and scent
work that has added to our understanding of how to work with our dogs—
thank you.

A salute is offered to all the hard working individuals who devote
time and effort as tracking test committee members, secretaries, tracklayers,
and judges. These folks remain the heart and life of this sport. Thanks to the
true experts on scent work, the dogs. Oh, how we wish we could experience
the world of their noses for even one day! They are our greatest teachers.

My training club, the Springfield Missouri Dog Training Club, has
a strong tracking interest. Members have earned over 140 tracking titles in
the last twenty-five years. The SMDTC club members with whom I have
worked most closely are Fran Ippensen, Laure' Young, Judy Asher, Tom and
Donna Hacholski, Joan and Lee VandenBerg, and Cathy Hawkins. Cathy
has been my partner in teaching many classes of tracking students. Kudos to
Rebel, Gunner, Poppy, Miss Kitty, Buddy, Carson, Happi, Ouijt, Bill, Coco,
Dodger, Deacon, Choctaw, Breezie, Reigel, Sara, Sassy, Chaca, Britta, Tori,
Dillon, Chelsea, Trapper, Rocky, Babe, BeeGee, Chrissy, and Fern and many
more dogs and owners who earned their "Ts" when the dogs were young
pups.

To the next generation of tracking dog trainers and their dogs, remember these words of wisdom…"sunscreen, good footgear, dress in layers,
and always carry plenty of water for the dog!"

WORKS WITH ADULT DOGS, TOO!

While my focus in this book is on puppy tracking, the techniques can work equally well with adult dog. It is, however, a bit more challenging to train an adult dog. The key is to give your adult dog a little more time to build his tracking confidence. Unlike a puppy whose mind is a relatively clean slate, an adult dog, especially one that has had lots of advanced training, may be mentally "locked in" to constantly looking to the owner for direction. This is terrific for many purposes, but it doesn't help a tracking dog develop the confidence to insist to a handler, "It goes THIS way buddy!" We simply have to convince the mature dog that he indeed is in charge and once you show him what to track he will learn to show you, the handler, the track and articles that are to be found

TABLE OF CONTENTS

1

AN INTRODUCTION TO TRACKING

WHAT IS TRACKING?

The tracking I will be teaching you and your pup involves the dog learning how to follow the ground scent left by a tracklayer along a pre-determined route. The tracklayer naturally creates a scent path along which the dog can track, be it around a field, across a parking lot, or along a road. Your dog's incredible nose—it has at least 300 times the scenting power of the human nose—gives the dog the innate ability to follow such a track, an ability you can enhance by learning the training routines and techniques laid out in this book.

WHY TRACK?

Tracking is great fun for both you and your puppy. For you, it offers a window into the mind of the dog. It's different from nearly any other aspect of training and living with your dog in that the dog is in charge. For the puppy, it develops his learning abilities, confidence and temperamental stability.

Tracking is a grand game for you and your dog. Once your puppy learns the "Find it!" game, it becomes one of the few areas of working and playing with your dog in which he gets to tell you what to do and where to go. When the dog or his owner needs a break from other training, a tracking session can perk you both right up. Tracking invariably helps the dog's mental/emotional development. I have seen shy dogs become confident. I have seen rowdy young dogs become steady and dedicated to the job of solving the tracking puzzle. It has shown me that mental exercise is just as important to a young dog's development as physical exercise.

At the human end of the tracking line, we must concentrate on things far removed from every day concerns. There are no IRS agents, bosses, or rebellious offspring in the tracking field. A friend says, "There is no such thing as a bad day tracking." Even if the tracking session does not go as well as planned, it presents an interesting puzzle for both of you to solve.

Tracking strengthens your relationship with your dog. Tracking success depends on concentrating on what the dog is communicating with his body language. This opens a new window in the human mind that leads to a deeper understanding of the "dogness" of our canine companions. On one occasion, I was able to use tracking training as a means to rehabilitate a dog that had become threatening to his owner due to a breakdown in the dog-owner relationship. That dog never earned his tracking title, but gradually he did regain his trust in his owner.

WHAT IS SCENT?

Every person (or animal) creates a certain level of scent as he moves about in his environment. Scent is defined in the dictionary as "a substance that affects the sense of smell." Skin cells constantly fall from our bodies and become part of the track scent. In addition, the pressure of footsteps creates a disturbance in the surface on which the footstep falls. On vegetated surfaces, scent is left on crushed vegetation when stepped on and becomes part of track scent. An example of this that humans can sense is the smell of a freshly mowed lawn or hayfield. But a dog can discern scent left by footsteps even on bare dirt or rocky soil. The scenting ability of most dogs is so acute that when checking out a newly encountered track, they can sniff a few yards in each direction and are able to determine which scent is newer and which scent is older. This allows them to discern in which direction a particular track goes.

My favorite way to illustrate scent is to use the following image as an example. Early in the morning, when I look at a dew-dampened lawn, I often see little happy trails criss-crossing it. These trails across the grass made by nighttime critters are briefly visible. Think of these as being scent trails. Both animals and humans create such trails of scent as they move across the landscape, but of course we humans almost always can't see or smell them. Dogs, however, have noses that pick up these scent trails to an amazing degree. Some dogs, like Bloodhounds, have an incredible ability to pick up scent trails even many days after they were created. On a warm, breezy spring day, my dogs sometimes lie on a hillside, nostrils flaring, reading scents from who knows how far away. I often wonder if they can scent the deer that live in the deep woods across the river from my house.

WHY TRACK WITH A PUPPY?

By seven weeks of age, a puppy's computer is totally switched on, but his brain is not cluttered with learned behavior. His attention span is short. If we make sure to not overtax the puppy's physical and mental stamina, he can learn more easily now than at any other time in his life. Thus I have found that you can begin tracking with a puppy as early as seven weeks of age.

The beauty of tracking training is you can begin any time you wish after the age of seven weeks. For example, one of my Dalmatians, Ch Paisley Poppycock CDX, TD (these initials denote that she eventually earned conformation, obedience, and tracking titles), began her tracking training at the age of eight weeks. She passed her tracking certification—a prerequisite for entering a tracking test (see Chapter 8)—four weeks later at the age of twelve weeks. To my knowledge, she is the youngest certified tracking dog of any breed. There was a tracking test in Iowa on her six-month birthday, the earliest a test can be taken. We entered, got into the test and drew the first track. It was December and the near freezing wind was blowing hard across the tops of those southern Iowa hills. I thought I could read on a few faces the thought that this little mite would never pass the test. Four adult dogs did not pass that day, but the diminutive Dalmatian pup did.

The point is that tracking is exciting no matter what age your dog is. I start my pups early because it is so easy and such grand fun to see them learn tracking. And if your goal is to earn the American Kennel Club Tracking Dog (TD) title with your puppy, you will have plenty of time to prepare. The official AKC definition of a puppy is under one year of age.

On the trainer/handler side, when training a young puppy, the mileage you will put on your walking shoes and the land required for training are both much less than with older dogs. Realize, however, you will always walk at least twice as far as your pup because you walk every track twice, once when laying it and again with the dog. Thus, you will become more physically fit yourself. Tracking is mentally refreshing to the person as well as the dog. I believe that by starting tracking early on with a puppy that partnership you form will be deepened in ways a non-tracker can not even imagine.

The lesson plans I present are a series of puzzles to solve each day. The stair-step approach develops intelligence, focus, and confidence. Tracking pups become excellent problems-solvers because they learn to solve problems early in their lives and they learn to work with a human partner.*

Warning…tracking is addictive for humans. Once the tracking bug bites, some never recover.

HOW DO YOU MOTIVATE YOUR PUPPY TO TRACK?

Which dogs make good tracking candidates? Just about any dog healthy enough to walk and sniff can learn to track. They seem to soak it up like little sponges. It is, however, easier to teach a puppy to track that is food motivated…a chowhound…a gravy gulper. If you have that rare puppy that doesn't care whether or not he polishes his plate, try to making sure he's hungry before you begin tracking sessions.

There are, luckily, motivators other than food. What does your dog love? Can you figure out a way to use what he loves as a tracking reward? A dog that loves to retrieve, for example, might find a ball or a toy a great motivator. A dog that loves to play tug may still be motivated by food drops but will enjoy finding a tug toy once in a while instead of a glove. Once you determine how to motivate your dog, he'll be a dandy advanced tracking candidate. The most advanced

---

*While the focus of this book is on puppy tracking, the techniques work well with adult dogs. See Chapter 9.

tracking dogs are article freaks and *live* to snatch up those gloves, wallets, combs, etc. that we use in tracking. I knew a Boxer who loved to pop balloons. She learned to track for a balloon reward. Now that's creative training!

Any healthy dog can track. The challenge is to get your puppy to track when, where, and what you ask him to track. Motivation is the key to success in tracking. You may be able to make a dog heel or gait properly, but you cannot force him to use his nose. You must make him want to use it when and where you ask him to.

WHAT KIND OF PERSON HAS SUCCESS AS A TRACKING TRAINER?

Can you walk? Can you see? Do you enjoy outdoor activities? Is it rewarding to spend time with your canine companion? Then tracking training is for you. It will teach you many lessons about your puppy's personality, how his mind and nose work, and brings the added benefit of being fun for both of you!

You can take the lesson plans and just go tracking casually and occasionally for the enjoyment of seeing the dog's natural abilities in scenting. If you do want to earn a tracking title, however, you must make a time commitment. You will likely have to invest several weeks of your time in this program. You may not have much free time left over for other hobbies for a while depending on how you and the puppy progress. I usually suggest to my students that they not continue with other dog training or competition during title-oriented tracking dog training.

Are you motivated enough to give this tracking thing a try? You can have success never tracking more than three days a week, but I think you and your puppy will have a much easier time and greater success if you can devote at least three or four weeks to tracking six days a week. Some lessons are finished in as little as 20 to 30 minutes. Some may take up to an hour. As the time between when you lay a track and when you work your dog on it increases, you may be able to run an errand or two and go back later with your pup. It is often easiest to fit tracking training into the longer daylight of summer

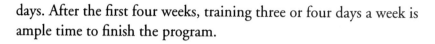

days. After the first four weeks, training three or four days a week is ample time to finish the program.

SETTING GOALS

My first goal in presenting this lesson plan is to enable dog and handler to attain the coveted American Kennel Club Tracking Dog title. Beginning trainers not only have to train the dog, but also must learn many new skills such as map making, line handling and the ability to read the dog. You may wish to try tracking just for fun and have no interest in earning a TD. That's fine. The lesson plans will work whether or not you want to win a title. Many years of experience in this sport have convinced me that nearly every dog/owner team can have an enlightening and exciting time tracking. You can even view it as part of an overall physical fitness plan for both dog and owner. We each must establish our own parameters for measuring our success.

My second goal is to present a tracking training method with enough clarity that those without a coach or an instructor can follow the plan successfully. While many people do their training with a group or tracking club, I am confident you can do this on your own with the information that follows. I once received an e-mail from a fellow who lived alone on 1,600 acres in the mountains in the eastern United States who said this method worked for him and his dog. So, whether you plan to compete in tracking or see this as a solitary pleasurable pursuit for you and your puppy, I am sure you can set and achieve your goal and have a great time!

2

GETTING READY TO TRACK

MENTAL AND PHYSICAL PREPARATION

Neither mental nor physical preparation is usually an issue for the puppy. Almost any normal puppy is mentally and physically fit enough for the lesson plan presented in this book. If there is any doubt about this, check with your veterinarian. Before you begin the first tracking lesson, teach your puppy to hunt out a very small treat that you drop right in the grass in front of his nose. Teach him the meaning of the word "cookie" or "treat" and teach this away from the tracking field.

Any person who is moderately physically fit should have no problem with entry level tracking using these lesson plans. You need to be able to walk several hundred yards a day and most people become more fit during tracking training. This is a real benefit. As mentioned earlier, the hardest thing for owners is that they must commit to finding the time for tracking and, more importantly, make a commitment to the mental effort to learn the handler's side of tracking. If you do, you will find teaching the dog the "Find It" game is the easiest part of the program.

THE TIME COMMITMENT

If you want to take your pup out and explore the world of tracking training in a casual way, bravo for that! Just try to follow along with the lesson plan and take as long as you like to complete the lessons. It may take you two or three weeks to complete one week as shown in the lesson charts. That's fine. Remember this should be easy and fun. This is a game for you and your dog to enjoy together.

For the highest probability of success in earning the American Kennel Club TD title however, I recommend you track up to six days a week for the first four weeks or until the lesson plan directs otherwise. This may seem arduous, but this frequency of training seems to help the dogs really "get it." Many dogs that do not train frequently enough early on begin to have problems when they attempt to work a track that is aged from 45 to 60 minutes, a problem noted tracking trainer Glen Johnson called "the hump." By this he meant that period in the age of the track when the scent of crushed vegetation in combination with the scent of body cells falling from the tracklayer seem to confuse the dog. Dogs trained by this method, i.e. six days a week, never seem to experience the difficulties of "the hump." Again, most sessions will take only 20 to 30 minutes. Some will take more than an hour. As stated earlier, if you can tough it out and track five or six days a week for at least the first four weeks of the program you will be more likely to succeed in earning a title if that is your goal.

TRACKING TEST SEASONS

Tracking test seasons generally are spring and autumn. Thus, tracking training time is usually during the winter and summer. When working with beginner dogs in the summer, especially during the first few weeks of training, try to track early in the day and avoid the heat. In the winter, track later in the day when it's warmer. Make it easy for your puppy, especially when working a very young dog. There will be time enough in later training to challenge the dog with temperature extremes.

FINDING LAND TO USE FOR TRAINING

There is no such thing as too much land for tracking dog training. I live in a semi-rural area and have permission to use several hundred acres of hay fields, woods, and wild areas that are close to my house. I obtained permission by going door to door with my tracking gear in hand (flags, harness, line, gloves, and clip board). I explain that I am training a dog for tracking. Most people assume that means search and rescue. If that assumption helps them understand and be willing to let me use their land, I just let their assumption remain intact. (*Yes,*

I know search and rescue is much more than just tracking.) If necessary, I explain I am teaching the dogs to follow the track of a person. I am careful to explain that while I do place flags along the track, *all* flags are removed an hour or two later after we are finished. I also make it clear that nothing is ever left in the field that might damage mowing or other machinery. I also tell landowners that the dog is always on leash or a long line and is never allowed to run free to chase livestock or wildlife. I offer to let landowners observe the training, but request that they not walk or drive on the track before I run the dog. I always take cooperative landowners food gifts at holiday time and I send a brief letter to each when my puppy earns his tracking title. That way, the landowner will be happy to see you when you show up to train for an advanced title with your dog.

If you have friends who own land, don't be shy. Ask them. If they are interested enough in the training, perhaps they will learn to lay track for you. It's wonderfully convenient to call a friend and ask, "Could you lay a three turn track in the alfalfa field at noon for me?"

Parks that are not heavily used by the public are excellent training grounds for beginning tracking dogs. Are the local soccer fields unused during the winter? Are there nature or wildlife conservation areas near you? Usually leashed dogs are allowed in these areas. Industrial parks often have large areas of unused land. When using non-rural areas for training, always carry plastic bags with you to pick up any doggie deposits. You will lose permission to use land if your dog's droppings make unpleasant surprises for others. Whenever possible obtain permission, but sometimes it's not possible to discover from whom you need permission for land use. In those cases I suggest going ahead and using the land, but be prepared to politely leave if requested to do so.

Do not use a field if it is freshly or partially mowed. Do not use land that shows a pattern of regular wheel tracks as this often indicates that agricultural chemicals or fertilizers have been recently applied. When obtaining permission, ask if there is a resident dog. If there is, that dog will probably resent any intruders on "his" territory and you probably ought to track elsewhere.

Be careful about using fenced land. This often indicates the presence of livestock on the land. Some cows, horses, geese or other domestic animals resent dogs. If you do enter a fenced area, remember this rule: *If a gate was open, leave it open. If a gate was closed, close it behind you.*

Sometimes rural or suburban churches own surrounding land for future expansion. Often you can obtain permission to use this land for training. Perhaps you could volunteer to help the church keep the land mowed.

TRACKING EQUIPMENT

Non-Restrictive Harness

A non-restrictive harness is one that does not interfere with the free movement of the dog's shoulders. Pulling harnesses that have a horizontal strap straight across the dog's chest are not good for tracking. Most dog equipment suppliers identify non-restrictive harnesses in their catalogs. For tiny pups you can make your own simple figure eight harness from big fat laces used with athletic shoes. I have made a leather tracking harness for older pups out of suede leather with the suede on the inside so it is non-irritating to the pup's skin.

Tracking Line

This line should be comfortable to your hands. I prefer a flat, woven, cotton line. For very small dogs or puppies, a line made of parachute cord (available at army surplus and outfitter stores) is ideal. It should be 40 feet long, with a snap on one end and no loop in the other end. I recommend you make a visible knot at 20 feet, as the handler is required by the AKC Tracking Dog test rules to remain 20 feet behind the dog. The easiest way to make the knot visible is to run some orange surveyor's tape through this knot and let three inches of the tape hang down on each side of the knot. Another way to make the 20 foot knot visible is to wrap it with brightly colored tape like blue paint masking tape. Tie additional knots at about 35, 36, and 39 feet. The function of these knots at the end of the tracking line is to allow you to realize, without looking down at the line, that the dog has

This is a non-restrictive harness; note how it does not interfere with the breathing or shoulder motion of a hard pulling dog.

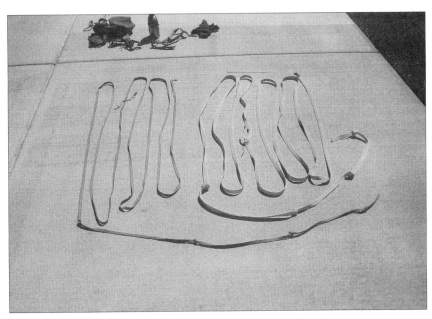

Tracking lines with knots tied at recommended intervals.

taken out nearly all of the line as he is searching for the track. Those knots signal the handler that he must make a decision about whether or not he should "step off" (go with) and continue to follow the dog. Is the dog tracking or not? If so, go! If not, then stand still and work the line back in to cause the dog to search in a smaller circle. You do not need to mark these end knots. Measure and cut the line for a 40 foot length after you have tied the knots.

Nail Apron (or belt with pouches attached)

Canvas nail aprons are available at nearly any lumberyard, hardware, or building supply store. If you have a military surplus store in your area, they often have canvas web belts with various sized pouches that may be attached to them. Believe me, you will need all the pockets!

Water Jug or Canteen

Get a canteen or jug that you can attach to your belt or stuff into your nail apron. Teach your dog to drink from your cupped palm or carry a drinking bowl with you. Collapsible fabric water bowls with plastic linings are great.

Zip Lock Bags

These are for the puppy's regular meal after you are done tracking. Moisten the dog's food with warm water and put it in zip lock freezer bags that are unlikely to leak. It's not fun to walk through a whole tracking session with water dripping down your leg, so check for leaks before you start!

All Weather Gear Including Boots

If money is no problem, Gore-Tex rain suits are wonderful. A rain hat and a long slicker type raincoat and some waterproof boots are minimum requirements. The rain gear should be somewhat oversized to allow for equipment and a clipboard to be tucked inside.

Clipboard

I recommend you carry a clipboard. If you train in a dry climate a covered one is nice but not essential—otherwise buy one with a cover. Attach a pencil or waterproof pen to the clipboard. You will track in

A nail apron or belt with pouches makes it easy to carry your tracking gear.

all weather with the exception of thunderstorms. Regular pens are not recommended because as soon as they get wet, or even slightly damp, the ink begins to run. You will need a supply of regular and waterproof mylar or waxed paper. If you are tracking with a friend, you may be able to split the cost of a roll of white butcher paper that you can cut to the right size for mapping. This holds up really well when wet. Mylar plastic sheets work well but are pretty expensive.

Track Flags
You will need 25 to 30 flags. These need not be as large as those used in tests. Locator flags used by phone and utility companies are inexpensive and work well in all but very hard or rocky ground. Contractor or surveyor supply companies have them. For hard or rocky ground you may need to buy some metal dowel rods and sharpen one end, bend the other end into an "L" or "U" shape and attach colored tape.

A variety of tracking flags.

Tracking Diary

A spiral notebook works fine. Your tracking diary will consist of your field notations and maps. Some trackers like to use a zippered notebook to protect their notes from rain. Attach a pencil with string or Velcro.

Treat Food

This is for food drops on the track. Be sure it's something smelly that your pup is crazy about. Many trainers use little slices of hot dog, cheese, or chicken liver. If ants and other "crawlies" are a problem in your area, then try putting food drops in little plastic camera film containers or very small snack size plastic bags.

Articles

For tracking articles use both brown cotton and leather gloves. Odds are good that one or the other will be the article used in a TD test. I suggest three pairs of cloth and one of leather. Occasionally use a wallet, shoe or sock, because although a glove is preferred, the rules allow some other personal article of the tracklayer's such as these. If a tracklayer comes back to the judges and discretely says, "I forgot my glove but I took off my shoe and left it at the end of the track," the judge will probably accept that as a test article.

Gloves for your hands

These are to protect your hands. If your dog is a fast tracker that pulls hard, I suggest weight lifter or cyclist gloves. The ends of the fingers are cut off and the palms are padded and come with both left and right hand gloves. They usually have a Velcro, snap or button wristband that allows you to attach them to your dog's harness between tracking sessions.

Tote Bag or Box

This is to keep all of your tracking gear together and is usually kept inside your vehicle. You never know when you'll find a new place to lay an interesting track!

Squirt or Spray Bottle

This is to wet down the dog in hot weather. If your dog is black or dark colored, working in the sun can overheat him quickly. While you should always carry water with you for the dog, in hot weather it's a good idea to also carry a squirt bottle to cool the pup. Spray his face, tummy, and the bottoms of his feet if he becomes overheated. Get your puppy accustomed to working a track while he is wet.

Sun Screen and Hat

These are for you, not the dog. The hat should be broad brimmed, suitable for sun and rain protection with a chinstrap or ties.

Bug Repellant

I don't use it. I don't want anything odiferous on me when I train a tracking dog. If you are going to use a repellant, be aware that the repellant scent will usually negatively affect your dog's scenting ability. Use it if needed on your ankles and wrists but try not to spray immediately before entering the tracking field *especially* with beginning tracking dogs. Use it judiciously. Never use it on the dog. He should already be on a flea and tick preventive program before you begin tracking training. Check him (and yourself) carefully for hitchhikers after each tracking session.

And don't forget the dog!

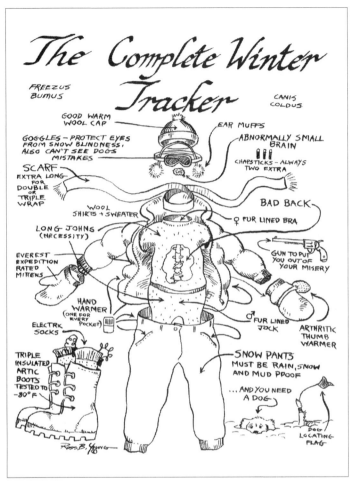

Do they make long johns for dogs?

WHERE AND WHEN TO TRACK WITH YOUR PUPPY

Try to use relatively clean tracking fields with fairly uniform type vegetation throughout the track. Wait at least three days before returning to use the same field or the same area of a large field again because you want a little re-growth of vegetation. When laying track, be mindful of the need to keep unused portions of large fields "clean." By clean I mean untracked so they will be available for subsequent tracking training sessions. Again, especially with a beginner tracking dog, allow a tracking field to "rest" for about three days before using it again.

When tracking a puppy, avoid ground cover higher than your knees. Also avoid fields with sparse vegetation, freshly mowed grass or extreme changes of vegetation. These are conditions in which tracking is harder because the scent is more difficult to follow. When tracking in extremely dry or sparse vegetation, the rest period before using the field again will need to be longer than three days to allow for re-growth. Tracking in light to moderate rain is fine for beginners, but avoid heavy downpours when working with an inexperienced dog. *Never track in thunderstorms.* Lightning is a killer. If you can hear *any* thunder, get out of the tracking field immediately.

As soon as your puppy becomes a confident, motivated, tracking dog (usually within three or four weeks), gradually expose him to the more challenging conditions I recommended you avoid in his early training. You may encounter any of these in a test.

3

TRACK LAYING AND MAPPING

TRACK LAYING

Our goal is to teach the puppy to successfully follow a line of ground scent laid down by a tracklayer. In training a beginner dog, the person who lays down the track is usually going to be doing it shortly before you ask the puppy to follow it. Very simply, laying a track for a puppy being introduced to tracking might typically involve slowly walking a route (thereby leaving a relatively heavy trail of ground scent) of about 30 yards. The tracklayer marks the beginning, the middle, and the end of the track with flags that are planted in the ground. The tracklayer can be you in this early phase of training.

Laying a track involves walking a route that you can map and exactly retrace. Since retracing your exact path is so important for training purposes, try to walk in straight lines. It's true that dogs can track curving lines with no difficulty, but curving lines are nearly impossible for the handler to exactly retrace. Be aware that it is very difficult to walk straight. Most of us have one leg slightly longer than the other or some other irregularity of stride that causes us to walk in curves, and if you walk long enough you may walk in a big circle! This is often seen by search and rescue workers trying to find those lost in wilderness areas. If, when you check behind you, you see you are walking in a curve, it will be necessary to add more flags as you continue that leg so that you will know exactly where you walked. Use as many flags as you need to during early training so you know exactly where the track is.

I suggest two manners of walking when laying track. Most of the time, you should just walk normally. Use your normal stride and call that a yard. Most people's natural stride is slightly less than a yard but it is close enough not to matter in training. The other manner of walking, shown on the lesson charts, is a "shuffle step." Drag your feet along the ground with a shortened stride. This makes a double wide track that is much more emphatic and obvious to the dog's nose. We use this when introducing a new element to the dog or to emphasize the track in a situation where the dog has experienced difficulty. This shuffle step walking style makes the track temporarily easier for the dog to follow. It takes about three shuffling steps to equal one of your normal strides so allow for this difference when measuring the length of the shuffle stepped portions of a track. I do a lot of "guesstimating" of distances when training my dogs—and it works well.

In addition, the tracklayer will drop food along training tracks at specified intervals. The tracklayer will also leave one or more articles that have his scent on them on the track. The most typical tracking article is a glove. You will always leave one article at the end of the track. As your dog gets more proficient, the tracklayer will add length, turns and increase the "age" of track, the age being the amount of time between when you laid the track and when your dog is asked to follow it. You will also find, as the lesson plan progresses, your dog will track more willingly without as many food drops.

A track laid for a beginning puppy might go something like this: Step forward from your starting point and plant your first flag. Stand there only long enough to sight where you will head and start walking in the shuffle step manner described above. Use at least two landmarks such as trees or buildings (one behind and one or two ahead of you) to help keep your track straight. Drop a food treat at the specified intervals in the lesson plan. Then typically you would plant a second flag 30 paces out, walk a couple more paces, drop the article, step on it, place food on it or in it, then continue several paces past the article and plant your final flag.

More complex tracks would be substantially longer and involve several turns and more variation in the vegetation. At the end of each "leg", you would typically plant a flag and then turn and take the track in a different direction (see the sample maps in the section on Map Making to follow.) As your dog progresses you will reduce the number of flags and food drops.

TRACK LAYING TIPS

- Place start and track flags slightly to the left of the track. Place corner and end flags directly on the line of the track. You will want to see and line up on them from a distance and be able to distinguish them from the start and track flags that are to the left of the track. Making this a consistent habit is important.
- Use two landmarks for each leg of the track. This will help you keep your track straight, as you want to avoid laying curved legs. Thus, at a corner you will have four landmarks, one in front, one behind, one to the left and one to the right.
- Look forward down each new leg before you step off.
- Before you step off on a new leg, look for landmarks that lie on or near the line of the new leg for your next turn, i.e., "I'm going to do a turn about 30 yards before that oak tree." If no such corner marks exist, be sure to note distant landmarks in at least three and preferably four directions at that turn.
- If you have great difficulty with field orientation and map making, build your skill by laying tracks with no intention of running the dog on them. Then see if you can walk the track without the dog after at least two hours.
- Continue to use a few extra flags as needed but try to get the flags off the corners as soon as possible. Some clever pups learn to visually run to the corner flags.
- When placing articles such as gloves on the track, walk several strides past the last glove, and then place an end flag directly on the line of the track.
- Separate tracks 30-40 yards (strides) to avoid cross track contamination.

FLAGS

Flags are used to provide information to the handler, not the dog. Use as many extra flags as you need during the early weeks of training. In addition, extra flags will prevent the pup from thinking each flag means a turn. Yes, some are so bright they figure this out very quickly. Count your flags and note their number and location on your map so that you leave with as many as you used. Remember to always obtain permission for the use of land for training and *never* leave any tracking flags in the field.

As shown on the charts, after Week 1 Day 4 you will always use a second start flag. This "two flag start" is used in TD tests. The second flag denotes the point before which you can ask the judge for a restart. After Week 4 of the training program you should be using only the start flag and the second start flag, 30 yards down the leg of the track. A caution: If you depend on the additional flags for too many weeks, a really smart wonder pup will use them as a visual clue and go from flag to flag rather than following the scent.

Always walk straight forward for several strides on the line of the track before planting the first start flag. Thus there will be a straight line of track up to the start flag. Some books suggest that you make a "scent pad" at the start flag by stomping about a one-foot square area with your feet. I do not recommend this as this is not how people walk in real life and it is never done at a Tracking Dog test. AKC rules state that the tracklayer is to walk normally up to and past the first flag.

Be consistent in placing track flags to your left when laying track. Corner flags and the end flag should be placed right in front of you, directly on the line of the track. This makes the corners and end of the track easier to sight on when keeping your puppy right on the track. After placing the glove at the end of a track, walk forward five strides before placing the end flag and note them on your map. Count these extra strides beyond the glove to the end flag and note them on your map. You must know *exactly* where the track(s) and glove(s) are.

Don't take your puppy with you while you pick up the flags after the lesson. Take off the harness and put him in the car or tie him up. You want him to earn the food only when he is in harness and tracking and he could find some undiscovered goodies along the way.

As you begin to run tracks with fewer flags, remember this advice: if you are not sure where the track is (and sometimes even when you are certain you know where it is) but the dog insists he's on the track, *go with him*. He may turn out to be wrong, but even if he is, he's tracking something. It's very easy for humans to become confused. You are trying to read the dog, handle the line, analyze the dog's tracking style, and keep in mind exactly where the track is. It is extremely de-motivating to the dog to be held back when he is on the track. It can destroy a dog's confidence. As a judge and a teacher/coach, I have seen many dogs just give up when they repeatedly showed their handler the track and the handler just wouldn't buy it. Remember if you need extra flags, use them. As soon as you can lay track well and correctly, start eliminating all but the start flags.

MAP MAKING

As mentioned above, one of the keys to success for a novice trainer working with a puppy is to know exactly where the track is. You have to know this so that if the puppy quits, gets distracted, or gets off the track, you will know exactly where to restart him. If you've never laid tracks before, you may be surprised how difficult this is. It is truly a learned skill. Thus, making good field maps and learning field orientation skills using those maps is a vital part of successful tracking training.

Make your own map for each tracking session. Note on the map any distant and corner landmarks, the number of flags used, and all relevant conditions including time of day, weather and specifics of location and vegetation on every track. Take a good careful look at your map before you start your puppy on the track. Remind yourself of the corner and distant landmarks as well as anything unusual you encountered in laying track. If you stood for a time on a corner or on the track while you chose landmarks or corner marks, your scent will have an increased presence there, so note it. On windy days that extra scent may make the corner a little more challenging for your pup. Don't worry, he'll figure it out.

Attach these maps to the diary where you add your post-training session notes. This will become a complete record of your tracking adventure with your dog. You will find this diary to be a tremendous help in figuring out what's going on when your dog has problems during a training session. It will help you answer questions such as, "Has he ever had trouble on hills before?" or "How much tracking has this dog done in high winds?" This diary will become a treasured reminder of a special time. You will study it often during training to learn more about your dog and his tracking style. As you add each day's tracking map, you should leave room in the diary for additional notes to be added later. I suggest leaving the back of each page blank for these additional observations. At the conclusion of the session, mark the dog's actual path while tracking on the map but use a different color ink or pencil. Do a brief write-up of the each day's training. I usually sit in the car and complete my diary entries before I leave the tracking site each day.

Before starting your dog on tracks with two turns, lay some practice tracks on which you will never run the dog. Use only the first leg start flags. Make good maps for these non-dog tracks. Can you go back in six to eight hours and walk them exactly? Put four quarters at different points on the track. Can you retrieve all four coins? Practice tracks with no corner or end flags until you can do this. Then run the dog on a fresh track with turns.

Here are three examples of actual field maps. Obviously, you don't need to be an artist to make these maps! The first map is the simplest, showing the layout of the track, the location of the flags and notations about the weather and vegetation. The second includes a number of landmarks that are helpful in terms of orienting yourself while on the track. The third is the same map as the second one but also shows the path the dog actually took. This actual dog track was added after the tracking session.

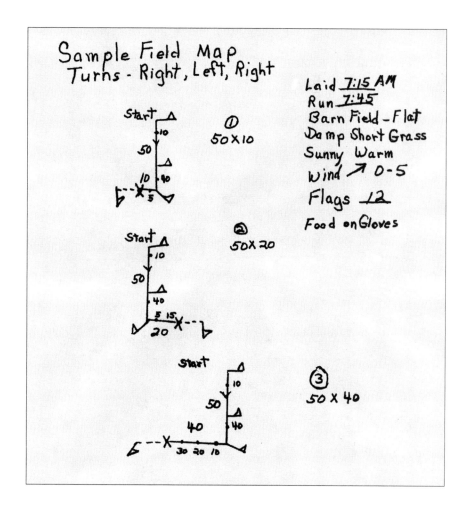

Sample Field Map
Turns - Right, Left, Right

Laid 7:15 AM
Run 7:45
Barn Field - Flat
Damp Short Grass
Sunny Warm
Wind ↗ 0-5
Flags 12
Food on Gloves

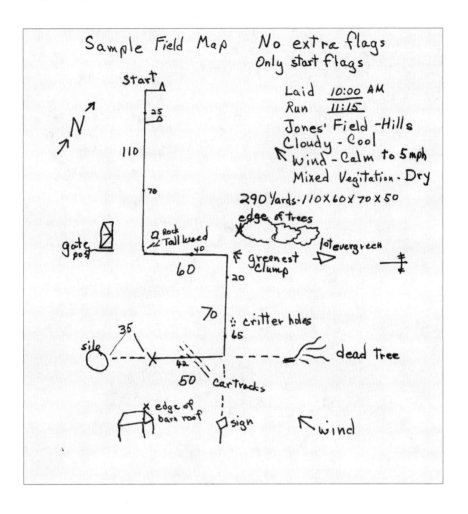

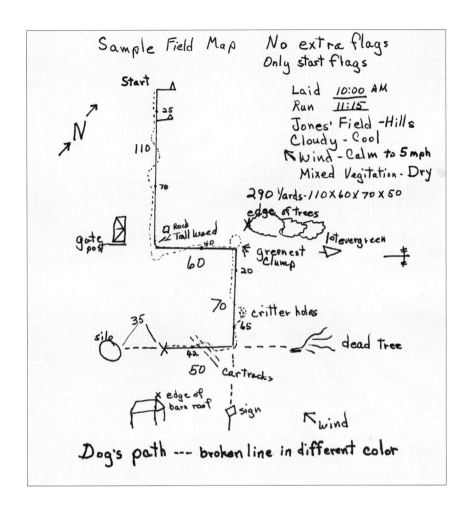

Sample Field Map   No extra flags
Only start flags

Start

N

Laid 10:00 AM
Run 11:15
Jones' Field —Hills
Cloudy - Cool
Wind - Calm to 5 mph
Mixed Vegitation - Dry

290 Yards - 110 X 60 X 70 X 50
edge of trees

25
110
70
35
gate post
Rock
Tall weed
40
60
20
greenest Clump
lot evergreen

70
critter holes
65

silo
35
42
50   Car tracks

edge of barn roof
sign

Wind

Dog's path --- broken line in different color

4

TRACKING
FUNDAMENTALS

TRACK AGING

The age of the track equals the amount of time between when the track is laid and when the puppy begins to work the track. You begin counting the age based on when you start to lay the track for TD training. Everything else being the same, the greater the age, the more difficult the track may become for your puppy. However, conditions may vary since the same field can change day by day or even during a single day. Be aware that many factors affect the apparent age of the scent on the track including:

> Time of day
> Wind
> Hills and valleys
> Ground moisture
> Barometric pressure
> Condition and height of vegetation
> Humidity
> Season
> Air pollution
> Pollens and dust

While all of these elements affect the apparent age of the track for the dog, this list is by no means complete. For example, a 30-minute-old track laid on sparse, dry vegetation, on hilly ground on a windy day may be a great challenge to a dog. Conversely, the same dog might be able to handle a two-hour-old track laid in a light mist on a calm day in lush vegetation as easily as a much fresher track.

Note in your tracking diary if your dog seems to have difficulty with tracks in a specific age range, or in certain conditions of terrain, wind, weather or other conditions. This will reveal situations for which your puppy needs more practice. Your tracking diary is the finest tool you have for problem solving.

Try to maintain the aging schedule (see Chapter 6) for tracks as shown in this book. Dogs seem to learn better and have fewer difficulties if we don't let them do too many tracks of the same age. So, if you only track once or twice a week, try to work the pup up to older tracks as you progress. Once the dog has experienced tracks an hour or more old, be sure to continue to work him on tracks 30 to 45 minutes old frequently. Don't get stuck in a rut by working tracks of about the same age for too long a period of time or the dog may assume that all tracks that you want him to follow are that age and fresher or older tracks may be a difficult transition for him to make.

STARTS AND RE-STARTS

Be consistent, start the pup the same way every time. First, throw the tracking line out behind you and clear any tangles. Attach the line to the harness. Put the harness on your puppy about eight feet back from the start flag. Grasp the top of the harness and physically take your puppy to the start flag. While holding the harness, tickle the grass above a food drop with your other hand and give your tracking command in a firm but pleasant, enthusiastic tone. My tracking cue is simply "Find it!"

When your puppy lowers his nose and leans into the harness, release your grasp on the harness, stand up, and let the tracking line slide through your hands and let him get on with it. In training you may have to repeat the tracking command several times at each start for the first few sessions. Don't let him just wander past the first start flag. Stop at the first flag. Wait beside your dog and hold him still until you see he's committed to tracking before you release the harness.

If he quits on the track for any reason during training, restart him. Take him to a "clean" spot exactly on the track; somewhere ahead of where he was tracking before he quit, where neither you nor he has walked. Then, start him again just as if from the first start flag.

Don't chatter at your puppy when he's tracking. Do not give your puppy obedience commands during the tracking session. Praise only when he finds or indicates at an article. If you use praise to tell him when he's on track, he'll probably form the habit of waiting for you to tell him where the track is the next time, too. He's not to focus on you, but instead focus on his job of following the scent path. You want your puppy to concentrate on tracking specifically where and when you tell him to "Find it!"

Do not be concerned if, at first, your puppy just runs to the end flags or the glove when it is visible. On future tracks there will not be an end flag and he won't be able to see the glove. He'll have to use his nose then. Right now he's just getting into "the game."

During the first two weeks of the training program, grasp the line about six to ten feet behind the dog in order to have better control and keep your puppy exactly on the track. Then gradually move your handhold on the line farther and farther back until you are holding the line at the required distance of 20 feet behind the dog. If the dog moves back toward you, stand still and take up the extra line. In a test, you are not required to back away from the dog, but you may not move forward again until your puppy is 20 feet ahead of you and actually tracking.

I do not recommend using a clicker to let your puppy know he is on track. You can't carry a clicker in a test and you wouldn't know where the track is or when to click during the test anyway. We do not ever want your puppy to become too dependent on any signal from you to show him the track. Clicker training, however, does have an application in tracking during "The Glove Game" (see Chapter 5).

ARTICLES

AKC tracking regulations state that the article should be a glove or wallet of an inconspicuous color. It need not be leather. Some clubs still use leather gloves as they make such a nice memento of a passing performance. You should use gloves made of cotton or leather since these are the traditional articles used in nearly all tests.

During training, always carry an extra glove with you in case you lose field orientation on the track. The glove you left at the end of the track may have been picked up and carried off by a passing human or animal. If you are in doubt about the track location, surreptitiously throw down the extra glove and then have a party with the dog when he finds it. You don't want to diminish the enthusiasm of a beginning dog because you made a tracklaying or map making error. After your puppy is tracking and retrieving gloves successfully, you should use an occasional wallet, sock, bandanna, hat or shoe. Tracklayers may use any of these as articles, or any personal article, if they have forgotten to carry a glove. Remember you cannot carry a glove or any other motivator with you in a tracking test. This would cause a judge to fail you for a handler error. Read the rules very carefully (see the Appendix).

Gloves are sometimes accidentally dropped on the track before the end by test tracklayers. It's wise, as your puppy becomes confi-

Look mom, I found a glove!

dent, to occasionally drop a second glove somewhere in the middle of the track. Tracking tests are often held on the same site year after year. Occasionally, you may encounter an old, forgotten glove from years before. See if he will continue to track after finding that first glove. There should be no extra glove in a TD test but, if he will continue tracking after finding a prematurely dropped glove, you may earn that TD title without having to run an alternate track later. These extra articles are also good preparation for advanced tracking, which includes more than one article to be found and identified by the dog.

USING FOOD IN TRAINING

I believe in using food to motivate your puppy to follow a track during training. I recommend that food be used at the beginning of the track, sporadically along the track, and then be placed on the article at the end of the track. These are referred to as food drops. Please note, however, that no food can be used in any AKC tracking test so, over time, we will need to "fade" the use of food in training a puppy to track. Fade means to use food less frequently as a reward over time.

Before your first tracking session, dump a little food out of the zip plastic bag you are carrying onto the ground and let your pup work to clean all the food out of the vegetation. I find this helps to keep him focused on finding goodies and other things with his nose.

Food drops on the track for a middle-sized puppy should be bites of food about the size of your index fingernail. In heavy ground cover they may be slightly larger. The food drop on the glove should be about the size of a quarter for a middle-sized breed. Food drops should be something really smelly that the dog truly loves, not ordinary dog food, perhaps small bits of cheese or hot dogs. Avoid crunchy treats, as we don't want the pup spending lots of time vacuuming up the crumbs. We want him to get onto the next treat quickly.

As you gradually fade the food drops off the track, you will probably find that the dog will track one or two legs without a food drop very easily. Retain the food drops toward the end of the track longer than any others. You want your pup to think that if he just keeps tracking a little longer, he might find a treat. Many pups love the tracking game so much that they quickly begin to overrun food drops anyway.

As your puppy grows, gradually shift some of the food away from his other meals into what I term the "tracking meal." The food the puppy eats during and at the end of his tracking for the day should be considered the tracking meal. If your puppy doesn't finish this meal, don't add extra food to his other meals. Your dog will not suffer depravation as long as he gets appropriate, nourishing food at his other meals.

Since tracking tests usually start early in the morning, training and feeding in the morning is wise, especially with a pup. When your puppy is ready for two meals a day, his larger meal should be the food he gets during and immediately after tracking with a light meal at the opposite end of the day. With a healthy pup, this should be the only food he gets. If your puppy has any health problems that might be affected by this regimen, follow your veterinarian's advice.

LINE HANDLING

A tracking line is many things. It is a tool. It is a communication line between you and your puppy. It is a device to allow you to test your pup's dedication to the track. It can be your best friend in a successful tracking effort or, if poorly handled, it can be a huge hindrance to your training and to your gaining understanding your dog's tracking style.

All line handling instructions are for right-handed folks. Reverse them for lefties. Line handling should be so well practiced that it becomes automatic. It takes a refined hand to hold the tracking line in such a way that allows good communication with a tracking dog. Clumsy line handling will interfere with the dog both physically and mentally. In addition, you have to keep your attention focused on the dog. Is he tracking right on? Is he confused and searching? Is he still working? Is he distracted? Is he at a corner or some kind of a cross track or an article? Ideally, once you have started the dog, you shouldn't have to look at the line except where it is attached to your puppy.

The second 20 feet of line represents a time bank in terms of when you must make decisions about whether to proceed and trust that the dog really is on track. It can be a huge hazard if you allow your own feet or brush or debris to become entangled in it. I express to my students that proper tracking line handling is, in a sense, like reading a book written in Braille. Learn to handle the line by feel, because you must keep your eyes on the dog.

The puppy needs to learn to track with the handler maintaining constant light tension on the line. If you allow a loose, lazy, droopy loop to form in the line, your puppy may get a very de-motivating, unintentional jerk just as he catches the scent and therefore might inadvertently quickly move off the track. Use the tension-release-tension line handling as described below to keep the puppy right on the track.

Mastering line handling is a key part of success. If you allow the tracking line to become slack between you and the puppy, or worse, let it lie on the ground, your puppy is likely to become tangled in the line. This can be distracting to the dog to say the least. While you reach down and untangle him you may unintentionally end up several steps off the track. You are allowed to call your dog to you to untangle him in a test, but if you do have to do this, you may be calling him just in the split second that he finds that new leg he was searching for. Thus, you may actually call him off the track, and by breaking his concentration, you may distract him and/or decrease his confidence in himself.

Any time you decide that the dog is not tracking, your feet should become like concrete blocks, heavy and not easy to move. Mentally nail your shoes to the ground until the dog takes out the line and tells you/shows you he's got the track. Then stand still and feed out the line as you gradually increase tension and you feel the dog tell you, "Here it is, come with me!" or see the dog's individual visual indications that mean, "Hey! I've got it now!"

I tell my students that every time their line touches the ground they should charge themselves a quarter and save the quarters in a jar. If your line handling is really sloppy you may at least collect enough money for a new dog toy or to make a donation to your local animal shelter!

In training, as your puppy gains confidence, try to handle the line as if you do not know where the track is. This is a tough mental task for the handler because you really must know exactly where it is. Exactly, in this case, means within six inches or so. Exactly means, "the corner is at precisely *which* yellow flower that's in line with which fence post, in front of which oak tree."

RIGHT HAND CONTROLS TENSION ON THE LINE

Hold the tracking line in your right hand with the right hand in front of your waist. To increase tension on the line, the right hand pulls directly back towards the handler's chest or waist. This gradually increasing tension should cause your puppy to swing right back on the track. As he does cross the track, release the line tension to show him the track. Do not pull to the right or the left to pull him back on track. The right hand elbow and shoulder control the amount of tension on the line. Keep your left hand low at your left side and grasp the line loosely with the left hand.

Demonstrating proper control of tension on the tracking line.

LEFT HAND CONTROLS EXTRA LINE TRAILING BEHIND

The left hand guides the line as it goes up to the right hand as well as controlling the extra line that lies on the ground behind or beside you. If the line becomes snagged in brush use the left hand to free it. You can do this without taking your eyes off the dog.

The left hand feels for the series of knots you have tied in the last eight feet or so at the end of the line. These end knots indicate the dog has pulled out nearly all the extra line, as when searching at a corner. Feeling these knots with your left hand lets you know, without taking your eyes off the dog, that you have to make a decision pretty darned quickly. Is the dog tracking, on scent, merely doodling around, working or not working? You can "ask" the dog by steadily increasing tension in your right-handed grasp. If he's on scent, ideally, he will tell you by increasing tension himself and moving off in the direction of the track.

If the line becomes slack, stand still as your right hand rises straight up in the air to keep the line off the ground. The left hand grasps the line directly below the right hand and pulls down to take out the slack in the line. Let the excess line "puddle" at your left side. Keep your eyes on the dog. Don't stand in the "puddle" of tracking line. In fact your feet should not be moving unless your dog is showing you he is tracking. Don't muck up the track with unnecessary footsteps. Don't step yourself into a tangle of tracking line.

A ROLE-PLAYING EXERCISE

Practice your line handling technique with a human partner taking the role of dog. Attach the line to your human partner's waist, not his neck, otherwise you may find friends very reluctant to join in this game! Smooth out your line handling by having your non-canine partner act out all the difficult handling challenges your dog specifically shows you during tracking. Does your puppy race madly about in circles at a corner? Does he quit if you put too much pressure on the line? Does he run straight back to you as if he wants reassurance? Learn how to deal with these line handling problems by using your human "canines."

I have seen dogs quit in seeming disgust if the handler's un-skilled line handling interferes with them too much. Some dogs will show you a turn once or twice and if you're not "buying it" they just seem to turn off. Others will track so fast that they may overrun corners. Have your human "dog" simulate your dog's style so that you may improve your line handling without confusing or abusing your puppy.

Then you take the dog's role for a while. Have your friend handle the line ineptly. Experience for yourself how really awful bad line handling is for the dog. The line should always have gradually increasing or decreasing tension with no laxity or jerking. I feel all tracking handlers should try this line handling role playing no matter what area of scent work, trailing, or searching you and your puppy may be destined for in the future.

FINISHING UP A TRAINING SESSION

When one training track is finished always remove the harness. When the harness is on the dog, that should mean "we are tracking." Put it back on at the next start. Yes, it's a hassle, but it's necessary. At the conclusion of a session you may remove the harness and attach the tracking line to your puppy's collar. Don't walk back through the area where you have just tracked. You don't want him to learn to backtrack for missed food drops.

As much as possible, be careful to save unused portions of large fields for subsequent tracking sessions. Laying a track, play time and games all contaminate a tracking field for at least three days when training a beginner dog or pup.

5

THE GLOVE GAME

The Glove Game is a very important part of the training program—unless, of course, you have that seldom encountered "Wonder Pup." A Wonder Pup is a natural retriever that always snatches the glove up in his teeth and turns to bring it to you. This is rare. Non-Wonder Pups, although they may love tracking, often will go right past the glove, even while still on the track. That's a big "oops."

The Glove Game is something you can start even before you begin tracking training. Whenever your puppy picks up something with his mouth, praise him lavishly. Yes, this means your underwear too. If you leave your underwear on the floor, then shame on you, not him! Try leaving a glove lying on the floor or in the yard. If he picks it up, praise and let treats rain down upon him. Have your own celebration, too. You have a Wonder Pup. The dog that is an article fanatic is a wonderful candidate for advanced tracking.

AKC tracking test regulations state that the dog must indicate (preferably pick up or touch) the article and the dog or the handler must retrieve it. Don't skimp on this article work. It's a real heartbreak for the handler, judges, and tracklayers when a dog does a great job tracking, but fails to indicate the article. Article work is doubly important for dogs who may continue to more advanced tracking. I train handlers to use positive reinforcement to get the dog to pick up the glove. We shape this behavior by rewarding small steps toward the behavior we desire from the puppy, called approximations. Thus, an approximation is when the dog gives an indication of interest in the glove, or any other behavior that indicates he is moving toward the retrieve of the glove, the goal of the Glove Game. This article work is critically important, but not based on any rigid time schedule. Bring your puppy along at his own pace. You can't enter a test until he is six months old so there is no need to rush.

USING A CLICKER TO TRAIN THE GLOVE GAME

The Glove Game is an ideal way for clicker trainers to utilize their skills in shaping behavior. The clicker is used to mark the behavior you will reward. That is, the behavior you want your dog to repeat. The "click" is followed by a reward. The "click" is an effective tool to help the puppy learn what he has to do to earn a reward. It is referred to as a reward marker because it "tells" the dog exactly what he did correctly. Your final goal in the Glove Game is for your puppy to avidly pick up that article, turn, and take at least one or two steps toward you. As soon as he is grabbing that glove, back up a few steps as you praise and you will get him to move toward you. Reduce using the "click" and begin to rely more on just praise once the dog is show-ing a willingness to grab the glove on his own, because a clicker or other motivational item is not allowed in a tracking test. Your voice is always with you and praising during a test is allowed. Advanced tracking handlers often have a little "praise-fest" at each article.

During the first week of training a quarter-sized food reward should be left on top of the glove. As the dog eats this reward, stand on the line and praise. When he has finished eating, remain standing on the line. Wait quietly with a treat in your hand. If the pup moves his nose toward the glove again, say "Good!" "Yes!" or click, then give him a treat. Wait quietly and hope for a repeat. If he doesn't return to the glove again within a minute or two, just take the harness off and go to the start of the next track. Perhaps he'll get the connection between glove and more goodies on the next glove.

We don't cue or signal the pup to pick up the glove. He must decide to pick it up himself. In any tracking situation the dog's job is to find things or people. In a test, part of the judge's job is to place the article so it is not visible from twenty feet away. It should be your goal to have the dog indicate the article himself while training so he will do it successfully with no assistance from the handler. You should always praise after he picks up the article, especially in a test. This Glove Game takes a lot of patience on the part of the handler. Personally, I think that simply doing nothing and waiting for the dog to figure it out is the hardest thing for most of us to learn. As one of my students said, "You mean I just shut up and wait?" "Yes, that's what I mean," I replied!

Play the Glove Game as part of the day's session whatever the dog's current level of tracking proficiency. If your puppy shows no interest in the glove, hold him at the glove until he does something as simple as just look at the it. Click and reward for looking at the glove. When the desired behavior is offered at shorter and shorter intervals, you can escalate the game to the next level.

TAKING THE GLOVE GAME TO THE NEXT LEVEL

If your reward timing is good, you should eventually see your puppy actually touch the glove with his nose. Nose touches (the target behavior) then can become the reinforced action. When the nose-to-glove touches become consistent and rapid, begin to shape the next stage of the behavior you desire. Now you should want something more than what he is now giving you. Possibly that he takes hold of the glove with his teeth. Then, raise the reward criteria again, i.e., the dog has to perform a more difficult task before being rewarded. The target behavior for reinforcement is now something more than just a glove touch. We hope he will grab at the glove or (Yippee!) pick it up. Whatever the targeted action is, watch for that action to be rapidly repeated as the dog figures out what you want him to do. Then raise the reward criteria again.

Use repeated small food reinforcements, instead of one large food treat. You want the target behavior repeated several times. Timing of the reward is critical. Have your food treats ready because a delayed reward while you fish around in your pocket does nothing to teach the dog the Glove Game; in fact it might confuse him and can really delay learning. Suppose he finally snatches that glove up and you are so surprised that you are slow in praising and rewarding that action. He will probably think you are looking for some other behavior, and it will be harder to get him to pick up the glove again. He'll probably offer several other less desired behaviors.

Integrate the Glove Game into your tracking training routine by sneaking several food rewards into your hand as your puppy approaches a glove on the track. The only thought you want in your puppy's mind at this moment in time is "glove + targeted behavior = reward." After several repetitions of the targeted response, remove the harness and go on to the next track. Learning comes through repetition of reward and praise. Larger food rewards but fewer repetitions of the sequence does not help the Glove Game progress as much as more frequent and smaller rewards.

During the second week of training, the larger quarter-sized food reward should be stuffed just inside the cuff of the glove. The pup can still get the food reward. As your puppy locates and eats the food treat in the glove, praise him. With extra goodies into your hand, stand on the tracking line to prevent him moving on past the glove and when he reaches the glove give him a "jackpot" with several treats. You want to build in your puppy the habit that stopping at the glove is an important part of tracking.

Your dog may go through a stage where he paws the glove instead of picking it up. This is a stage you may reward, but the next level should involve mouth-to-glove contact.

MORE GLOVE GAME TIPS

- Push food into the glove, but the dog should still be able to get the food out with a little effort. Reward all glove touches.
- Reward if your puppy grabs the glove with his teeth after eating the food inside. Reward additional grabs.
- Push food deeper into the glove to get your dog to pick up the glove even if just for a second. Reward additional glove pick-ups.
- Place food so deep into the glove that your puppy cannot get it out. Reward all glove pick ups.

- From this point on, work toward having the dog pick up the glove and turn toward you, then take a step or two toward you with the article in his mouth.
- If the dog seems well focused on the glove, discontinue leaving food *in* the glove.

You and your dog will not necessarily follow these steps exactly as described above. The levels of the Glove Game are simply approximations of the desired behavior and these may take many forms depending on your puppy's creativity. Some of the things the pups do at this point are hysterically funny and it is intensely interesting to see their little minds at work.

At home, praise the dog anytime he picks up anything. Without the dog watching you, try leaving several random gloves in the yard or house. Be prepared with a pocket full of treats. Let your puppy into the area and just watch. Do not give any retrieve command. When he indicates or, hallelujah, picks up a glove, click or praise and reward. If you run out of treats, end the game. Put your puppy away and pick up any remaining gloves.

The Glove Game is goal oriented and goes on throughout tracking training. Usually pups are picking up and bringing the glove by the fifth or sixth week of training. Some catch on a little more slowly. If you have done a good job of reinforcing the glove pick up, the lack of food on or in the glove will make no difference to the pup. If it takes a little longer to reach your goals or you have to keep placing food in the glove a little longer, don't worry; he'll get it eventually.

If your dog just will not retrieve the glove, then teach him to lie down at an article. Make sure you have taught him a good, solid, positively reinforced response to a down command while at home. Don't try to teach the down as part of a tracking session. Next, when he reaches the article, stand on the line to stop him at the article. Give his down cue. Praise and reward lavishly.

When you reach the point that you are no longer leaving food in the glove, buy some new, non-food scented gloves. The gloves in a test will not be impregnated with the scent of food. As the puppy advances in his article work, occasionally leave a non-glove article at the end of the track as you may encounter something other than a glove at a tracking test.

Annie the puppy succeeding at the Glove Game.

6

A LESSON PLAN FOR YOU AND YOUR PUPPY

WEEK 1

Now that you understand the basics and the terminology, here is a detailed six-week lesson plan for you and your puppy. As you move forward, the lengths and layouts of the tracks will become more challenging and the age of tracks will be increased gradually.

During the first week allow the pup to watch the tracks being laid out and run the pup on all the tracks immediately after laying them—as little aging as possible. If you are laying the track yourself, you will need to tether your pup near the beginning of the first track. You may even have to tie him to the car door or bumper if no tree or bush is conveniently available. Some of my students tie their dogs to a corkscrew device that screws into the ground. If at all possible, try to have a helper lay tracks for you during these initial lessons. In any event, it is important that your pup see the track laid during early training sessions. The handler is not to talk to the dog while laying the track. You want your puppy's entire focus to be intensely on what is happening with the tracklayer (whether a helper or you) out ahead of him.

To help the puppy focus on the tracklayer, the *handler* is to hold the pup while the tracklayer teases the puppy with the word "cookie" or "treat" or whatever word means a food goodie to this dog. While laying the track, the tracklayer is to repeatedly twist his body back—but *not* move his feet—and tease the pup visually and verbally from a distance. This will help keep your puppy's attention on watching the goodies being placed along the track as it is being laid out.

Note that if you are laying the track yourself you will be performing this routine while the pup is tethered where he can watch you. Keep this routine up for the first three days, or longer if needed, to maintain your puppy's interest in the track.

Put the harness on the pup about eight feet behind where the tracklayer will place the first flag. If you have a helper laying track for you, after he finishes laying the first series of tracks as shown in the chart for that day, he should walk straight ahead for about 20 strides and get out of the pup's sight. If he can't get out of the pup's view, he should sit or crouch or lie down and not move or make any sound. At this point, you don't want your puppy visually stimulated; you want him using his nose.

Track the pup on a six-foot lead or hold the tracking line at about six to ten feet during the first week. This will allow you to keep him right on the track. This means right in those footsteps. Keep light tension on the line at all times. If the pup veers off the track, gradually increase line tension by pulling straight back on the line. When the tension causes him to swing back toward the track, release the tension just as he crosses the track. This is sometimes referred to as "dumping the dog's nose down the track."

Do not pull toward one side or the other and don't lean to one side or the other to get the dog back on the track. This turns into a handling fault called "guiding the dog." In a test, it's considered cause for the judge to fail the team, especially if the track is visible. Besides, most of the time in a test or in real life situations, you will have no idea where the track is and you'll probably misguide the dog. Build good handling habits from the beginning.

WEEK 1 TIPS

- At the end of each line of track, stop your pup at the glove. As your puppy finishes eating the food on the glove, praise him as you kneel down beside him and remove the harness. Attach the leash to his collar, stand up and take him to the next start. He needs to learn that any time the harness is on he should be thinking about tracking.

- All tracks are to be laid into the wind this week. For the first two days leave a large food reward on top of each glove.
- Starting the third day, stuff the food reward just inside the cuff of the glove. You want him to dig at and mouth the glove to get the food.
- It's best if you have a helper to lay the tracks this week. If no help is available, tie your puppy to a stake or tree near the first start flag while you lay the tracks. He should be directly behind the line of the tracks where he can see you laying the track.
- The tracklayer should use a shuffle step stride for the first practice tracks.
- Stick to the food drop schedule as shown in the lesson plan charts.
- Don't be concerned if your puppy overruns some food drops on the track in order to get to the glove. That's normal.
- Try to keep him down to a fast walk or a slow trot. You don't want him racing down the track. The super-fast tracking dog is very hard for his handler to read.
- If your puppy stops to sniff out and find every food drop, that's fine, too. That means he'll be a dedicated and deliberate tracker.
- Draw your own tracking map for each day's lesson. It's good practice for developing your map making skills. Attach these maps to your tracking diary. Note date, location, time you begin to lay track, time of day, weather and temperature, ground conditions and landmarks. Study the sample maps included in this book.

UNDERSTANDING THE LESSON PLAN CHARTS

Tracking charts are NOT drawn to scale, nor are the charts the same scale throughout the book.

◀ Flags.

☆ Food drops. In the early weeks of training, place food drops to the immediate right of the start flag, the rest of the food drops should be exactly on the track. *No food drops at any other flag.* After several weeks of raining, make the transition from leaving the first food drop sometimes right at the start flag and sometimes farther down the first leg of the track as shown in the lesson charts.

☆ Articles (gloves). Place a generous — about quarter-sized — food drop on the glove.

⇐ Wind direction. Check it every time you lay a track.

═ A double line indicates a shuffle step lay of track. Each foot scoots forward six inches at a time, shuffling, scuffing and stamping the track into the vegetation. Keep your feet fairly close together. I prefer this to the traditional double laid track where the tracklayer walks forward and then returns back up the same track.

─ A single line indicates a single lay of track. Walk normally. Do not stretch out your stride to try to make it equal a yard. For training purposes consider a stride equal to a yard even though it really is not.

• Charts with practice tracks in a straight line include articles (gloves with generous food drops) placed strategically along the track to motivate your dog. These are short, separate tracks laid in a straight line with a gap of about 10 yards between the glove at the end of each track and the beginning of the next track. A separate end flag is not needed when the tracks are extremely short. As the pup completes each track, either pick him up and carry him to the next start flag or take the tracking harness off, attach the line to his collar and lead him to the next flag in the series. After the puppy finds the final glove, on the final track of the training session, dump the pup's meal on top of the glove and praise him as he enjoys it.

• Tracks should be separated 30-40 yards on either side to avoid scent contamination on parallel tracks.

WEEK 1

Lay tracks this week in long straight lines. Place all start flags to the left of the track. Place food drops directly to the right of start flag, and exactly on the track at 2, 4, 6, 8 yards (if necessary) and on the glove. All tracks this week are "lay and run" tracks. Do not wait in order to age the tracks this week. Lay tracks keeping 30-40 yards separation between them. Food drops, articles, flag locations, wind direction and length of track are noted.

Here are a series of tracks for you to lay and practice with your puppy during Week 1.

WEEK 1 DAY 1

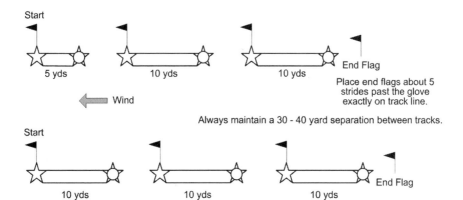

WEEK 1 DAY 2

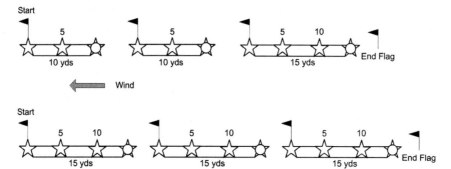

WEEK 1 DAY 3

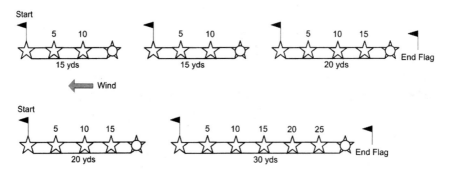

WEEK 1 DAY 4

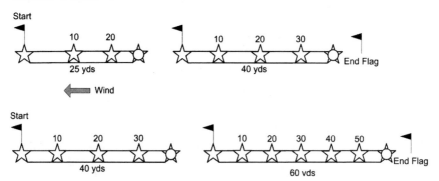

WEEK 1 DAY 5

Begin to use single laid tracks on your third and fourth track for the day.

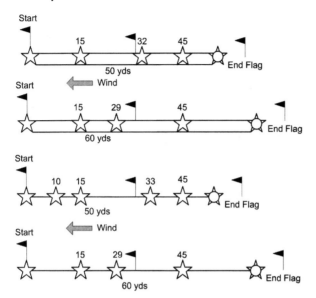

WEEK 1 DAY 6

As the length of tracks increase, you may find it difficult to lay them in a straight line. Use extra flags as needed.

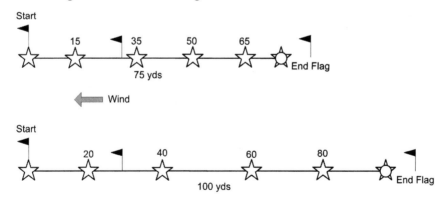

WEEK 2

The training tracks used during Week 2 are similar to Week 1. Now you will begin to run single laid tracks consistently with the wind at the dog's back. Also, you will begin to age the tracks during this week instead of running them immediately after they are laid. Age of the track for TD level work is counted from the time the tracklayer *begins* laying track, not when the tracklayer finishes. Here is the schedule for increasing the age of the practice tracks during Week 2:

Lesson	Age of Track
Week 2, Day 1	5 minutes
Week 2, Day 2	10 minutes
Week 2, Day 3	15 minutes
Week 2, Day 4	20 minutes
Week 2, Day 5	25 minutes
Week 2, Day 6	30 minutes

WEEK 2 TIPS

- If you deviate from the age of track schedule, go back and pick up where you left off.
- Use the 40 foot tracking line the second week and try to stay at least ten feet behind the dog. Use the "tension increase, tension decrease" method of handling the tracking line.
- As stated earlier, don't let the pup run down the track. Anything from a deliberate walk to a slow trot is desirable. Both you and your puppy need to develop good habits from the beginning, as that will contribute to your success later. A hard charging dog often overruns turns and may lose the track.
- Your puppy is allowed to see the tracks laid during Week 2, but is no longer teased by the tracklayer.
- Draw your own tracking map for each day's lesson and study it.
- All tracks will be single laid in Week 2. Walk normally. Count a stride as a yard.

- All tracks during Week 2 are laid with the wind at your back. If there is no measurable wind, just go ahead and track. If the pup does not gain enough experience working scent in wind now, you should go back and do some remedial work tracking in wind later.
- Increase the age of track five minutes each day during Week 2.
- Continue to stuff the bigger food reward into the cuff of the glove. Place it a little deeper into the glove this week. You want your puppy to dig and work at the glove to get the reward. You want to ensure that the dog *stops* at the glove. The track does continue on as the tracklayer walked off. Some dogs become intoxicated with tracking and blow past the article. Hold firm or stand on the line for a minute or two with your puppy at each glove and praise lavishly. This holds him at the glove.
- Be quiet and see if he touches the glove again. If he does, praise and reward. Will he touch it a third time? Be still and wait a few seconds. If so, praise and reward; if not just take the harness off and go on to the next track.
- If your puppy happens to pick up the glove with or without having eaten the food inside it, jackpot him with an extra food reward and praise. If the pup does not pick up the glove this week, maybe next week he will. Do not give him a retrieve command to get him to pick up the glove. You won't be able to do that in a test so don't do it now. He must learn to identify and pick up tracking articles without any cue from you.

WEEK 2 DAY 1

During Week 2 all tracks will be single laid and the dog will track with the wind at his back. Begin to run tracks according the aging schedule above.

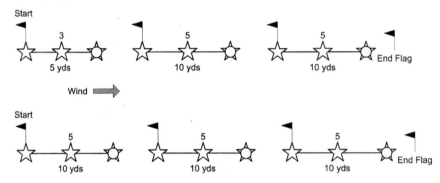

WEEK 2 DAY 2

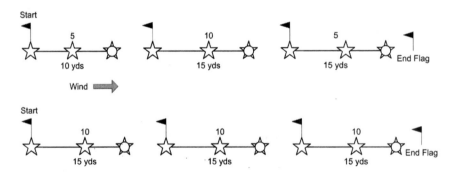

WEEK 2 DAY 3

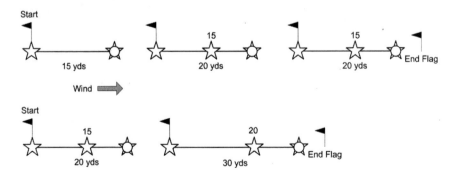

WEEK 2 DAY 4

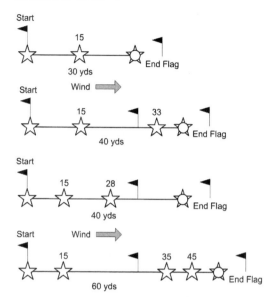

Start
15
30 yds
End Flag

Start   Wind ➡
15   33
40 yds
End Flag

Start
15   28
40 yds
End Flag

Start   Wind ➡
15   35   45
60 yds
End Flag

WEEK 2 DAY 5

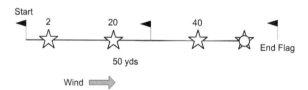

Start
2   20   40
50 yds
End Flag

Wind ➡

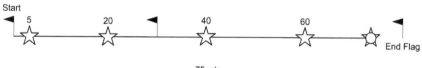

Start
5   20   40   60
End Flag

75 yds

WEEK 2 DAY 6

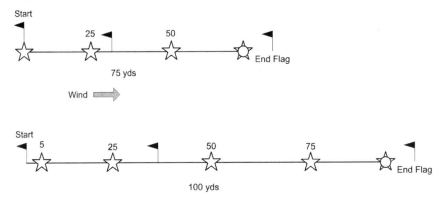

WEEK 3

Now it's time to start training in crosswinds in addition to tracking into the wind. Each track is to be 50 yards long (100 for mature dogs), separated by at least 40–50 yards. You may lay tracks back and forth across a field just as long as each track is in a crosswind. Use extra flags if needed.

By the third week of training, no longer allow your puppy to watch the tracklayer walking the track. After completing crosswind work, note the wind direction and estimated speed on *all* your track maps. You want to be aware of how well your puppy is handling tracking on windy days, especially in hilly terrain. Is there an area near you where there are more winds due to hills or ocean or lake breezes? Good, use that. Be aware that wind can do some unusual things to track scent especially when combined with hills, valleys, sources of moisture, trees, or buildings. You should have some interesting entries in your tracking diary after you and your puppy work crosswinds.

Here is the aging schedule for Week 3:

Lesson	Age of Track
Week 3, Day 1	15 minutes
Week 3, Day 2	30 minutes
Week 3, Day 3	40 minutes
Week 3, Day 4	45 minutes

Week 3, Day 5　　　　　　　50 minutes
Week 3, Day 6　　　　　　　30 minutes

In training the pup to handle crosswinds, the lesson plan is goal oriented. The pup is to learn to stay right on the track no matter what the wind situation is. This rarely takes more than a few days. Lay four tracks each crosswind day as shown in the lesson charts.

It is important to teach the dog to handle crosswind tracking before beginning work on turns. Try not to train inexperienced pups in high winds, that is, above twenty-five miles per hour. Even mild breezes at three to five miles per hour will help your puppy learn how scent behaves in wind. Do as many crosswind tracking days as needed by your dog. If your pup has trouble following a crosswind track, try training on a few tracks that are 15-30 minutes old and then begin again gradually increasing the age of the tracks.

The puppy may only want to track into the wind, but don't allow that. Continue working on crosswind tracking in straight lines until the pup handles it well. Some pups learn this crosswind tracking very quickly, some take the whole six days. A good test is to lay a track across the top of a rise during a moderate to strong wind. The wind will blow the scent off the top of the high ground. This is a true scenting obstacle, but you may encounter it in a tracking test, so make sure your puppy can understand and deal with it. Some dogs seem to panic when they lose scent in windy conditions. This tends to make them work faster and faster in an extreme effort to find the track scent they have lost. Try to keep the dog moving slowly enough so he can concentrate and scent better. Additionally, a dog racing around is very difficult to read and panting can impair his scenting ability; if this happens in training, try calling him to you and offering him a drink of water. This short break may help him work more calmly when you re-start him.

WEEK 3 TIPS

- When training for crosswinds, use extra flags to help you know exactly where the track is.
- Make sure that the tracks are separated at least 40-50 yards on either side.
- Walk well past each end glove and don't let your puppy track beyond the end glove or between the tracks.
- Remove the harness between tracks and walk him to the new start with the line snapped to the collar. If your puppy is small enough, you may leave the harness on and carry him between an end glove and the next start. If his paws are on the ground and he's got his harness on he should be thinking, "Oh boy, I'm goin' tracking now!"
- As you will be going back and forth in parallel lines, mark your path *between* tracks on your map. It's very easy to get confused when you go back to run the tracks with the dog. Check your maps carefully before you begin the training session.
- Be sure you have an extra glove. If you become confused about where the track is, throw down the glove and party with the dog. Then go home and start the same lesson over again the next day. Resolve to do a better job laying track and memorizing the track the next day. Always give your map a last quick look before you get your puppy out for the session. The lesson for that day may have been how important it is to make a good clear map and study it just before every training session!
- As always, give your puppy his meal at the last glove of the session.

WEEK 3 CROSSWIND TRACKS

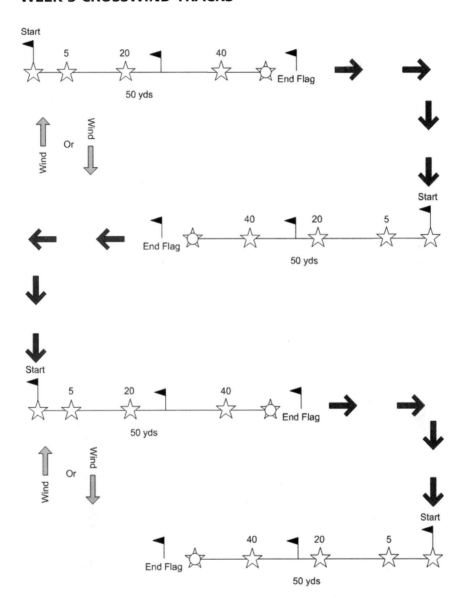

WEEKS 4-6

Continue training according to the charts for succeeding weeks. Be careful about spacing your tracks well apart. This separation should vary with the strength of the wind on that day; a larger separation is needed when crosswinds are stronger. You don't want your puppy to scent one track when he is on another. You will also start adding turns to the tracks in this time period.

Lesson	Age of Track
Week 4, Day 1	55 minutes
Week 4, Day 2	60 minutes
Week 4, Day 3	1 hour & 5 minutes
Week 4, Day 4	1 hour & 10 minutes
Week 4, Day 5	1 hour & 15 minutes
Week 4, Day 6	30 minutes
Week 5, Day 1	1 hour & 20 minutes
Week 5, Day 2	1 hour & 25 minutes
Week 5, Day 3	1 hour & 30 minutes
Week 5, Day 4	1 hour & 35 minutes
Week 5, Day 5	1 hour & 40 minutes
Week 5, Day 6	30 minutes
Week 6, Day 1	1 hour & 45 minutes
Week 6, Day 2	1 hour & 50 minutes
Week 6, Day 3	1 hour & 55 minutes
Week 6, Day 4	2 hours
Week 6, Day 5 +	Vary age from 30 minutes to 2 hours

After reaching the point where you run a two hour old track, vary the age of the tracks between 30 minutes to an hour and a half. Occasionally run a track that is two hours old. Practice plenty of tracks that are from 30 minutes to one hour old as that is what you usually encounter in a test. Dogs that have primarily been trained on tracks two hours old and older frequently have trouble following a fresh track. There seems to be too much scent and the dogs become confused.

If your puppy has a problem at one training session, he may just be having an off day. Note all conditions and circumstances and the fact that the day was less than successful in your tracking diary. One bad day does not necessarily mean there is a problem. Your puppy may do just fine the next day. Having two bad days in a row probably indicates a problem.

The first potential problem to consider at this point is the impact of the wind. If your puppy is having a problem on turns, lay a few tracks with the wind blowing in his face as he makes the turn. The wind will be blowing the scent of the second leg into his nose. Then go back to the regular program and lay track without regard to wind direction.

If you think that your puppy doesn't like tracking with a wind in his face (which may show up this first week of work on turns) use more frequent food drops on the leg of the track that turns into the wind. If the problem persists, your job is to figure out what new part of the tracking training is proving too difficult. Is the pup healthy? Is he motivated? If the dog is losing motivation, the answer may be that you have given him too many variables at once. It could be that your handling skills need improvement. Are you communicating well with the tracking line? Was there a weather change that confused the dog? Going from dry to lush vegetation is just as big a challenge to your puppy as going from fresh green vegetation to dry, sparse fields. Your diary holds the key. Study that diary.

Always note the tracking conditions, especially wind speed and direction on your maps as you lay each track. Yes, wind direction and speed on each track, since wind can change during the course of a tracklaying session. Check it again before you run the dog on the tracks. Note on your map if the wind changed between the time you laid the track and the time your puppy was run on the track. Study your maps carefully to discern if the pup has trouble handling wind. Was it suddenly sunny after along spell of cloudy weather? Was this a new field? What was different?

If you encounter situations in track laying that may prove an obstacle for your puppy, use extra food drops, especially just past the obstacle, to help the puppy learn and be rewarded for his persistence in tracking. Examples of this type of obstacle are critter holes, car tracks or small dips in the terrain that may be animal runs.

Continue to focus on learning to read your dog. Begin to note on your maps what your dog does when he loses scent at a corner. When he realizes the track is no longer in front of him, what does he do? This is called a "loss of track indication." What does he usually do when he reacquires the scent? You must learn to recognize these indicators. At this point in training, you should be well on the way to becoming skilled at reading your dog and learning his tracking style.

Try to keep the dog moving slowly and steadily as he approaches a turn. You want him to track all the way up to the turn. It's very easy for a fast tracking dog to really overrun a turn. Curb this tendency in the early training. Some dogs may panic at the loss of scent on a turn. Don't let your puppy get into the habit of racing madly around in a circle as he searches for a new leg. If this happens, you will find it useful if you move your grip on the tracking line up to about ten to fifteen feet from the dog for better control as the dog works out the turn and finds the new direction of the track.

WEEK 4–6 TIPS

- Make the Glove Game (see Chapter 5) part of the regular tracking training session.
- Use the same charts for training Day 1 and Day 2 this week. The only difference will be the direction of the turns. On Day 1 do a right turn track, then a left turn track, then a right turn track. On Day 2 simply reverse the direction of the turns.
- Tracks will be single laid or shuffle step laid as shown on the charts.
- On Day 4 repeat the chart for Day 3 but reverse the direction of the turns. Since you have already given your puppy the experience of tracking in a crosswind, you may lay tracks this week without regard to wind direction.

TRACKS WITH ONE TURN

As soon as you are able, discontinue the use of extra track flags, corner flags and end flags. Be sure to note landmarks carefully on your maps.

WEEKS 4–6 DAY 1

Use a shuffle step on the second leg of the tracks after the turn.

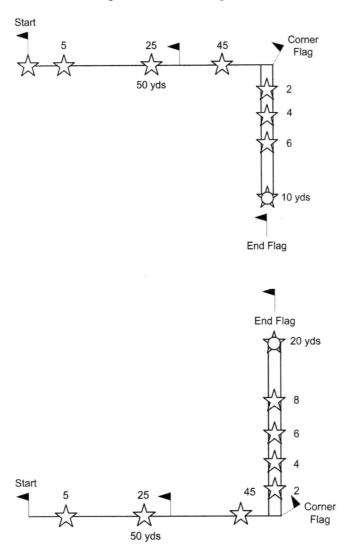

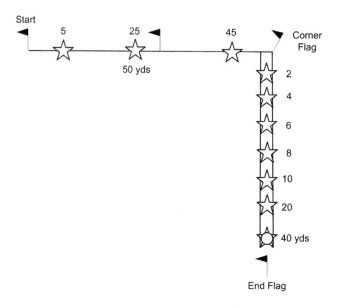

WEEKS 4-6 DAY 2
Use the same tracks as Day 1, but reverse the turns.

WEEKS 4-6 DAY 3
Lay tracks with one turn, single laid throughout.

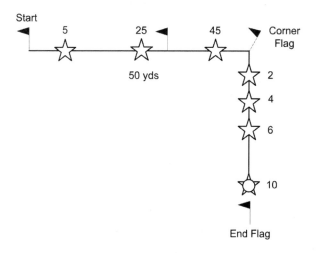

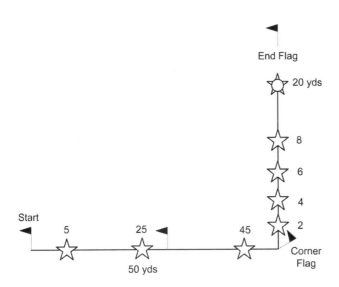

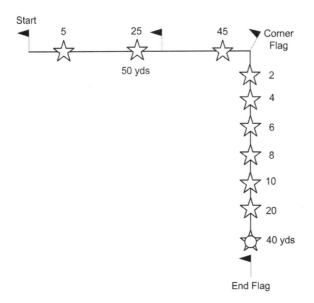

WEEKS 4-6 DAY 4

Use the same tracks as Day 3, but reverse turns.

WEEKS 4-6 DAY 5

Begin to train on tracks with two turns. For puppies, two turn tracks should be 50 x 50 x 50 yards; for adult dogs 100 x 100 x 100 yards. Continue noting landmarks and corners on your maps. Use a start flag and a second start flag at 30 yards. You may use corner flags also. Each day's lesson for a week will be a two turn track.

After a week of two turn tracks he'll probably be able to successfully complete a week or so of three turn tracks. If he can do three turns, he can probably do four turns. Now the training becomes very interesting and your diary entries should become more detailed. Start reducing the frequency of the food drops. Retain food drops on the last leg of the track longer than any others.

You may use corner flags and end flags also if still needed. Soon you must learn to lay tracks and make a map without the help of corner flags. Before you ever run a puppy without corner flags and end flags, test your mapping skills and field orientation. Lay a four turn

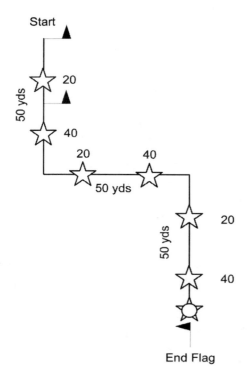

track using only the first two start flags. Go back several hours later and walk the track exactly. You will be surprised at how difficult this is to do. Do not run the puppy on this track.

WEEKS 4-6 DAY 6

Use the same track as Day 5, but reverse the turns.

READING THE DOG'S BODY LANGUAGE

You must be able to read the dog's body language visually and to feel it through the tracking line. You won't have tracks marked with those convenient flags forever! You won't always be the one laying the track for your puppy.

When you recognize a loss of track indication, *stand still and feed out the line until you see the dog indicate the new leg.* When you see your puppy recognize and take the new leg, watch carefully and feed out a little line. Once you feel the knots signifying the end of the line, you must make a decision. Is he committed? If so, step off in the new direction following the pup without jerking the line. Retrieve the length of the line steadily, with no jerking, until you are holding it again at the twenty-foot knot. Do this as quickly as you can to be prepared to repeat all of this at the next turn. The next turn may be as close as 50 yards ahead in a test.

Remember that in a test you must remain at least at the 20 foot marker on the tracking line unless the dog runs toward you causing you to take in extra line. In a test you are not required to back away from the dog, but do not move forward unless the dog is at least 20 feet or farther ahead of you. If the dog moves toward you, stand still and keep the line up out of the dog's way. Wait for him to show you the track. You may only advance down the track when the dog is actually tracking and is 20 feet ahead of you, so be especially careful about this if the track in a test is visible to you. If you do advance down the track without the dog taking you down the track, the judges must fail you for guiding/aiding the dog. This is why, from the very beginning, you only apply tension to the line by pulling back directly toward the handler, not to the right or the left.

An exception to the "20 feet from the dog rule" is that you may call the dog to you to untangle him from the line. Be careful about doing this because you don't want to call him just as he simultaneously picks up scent at a difficult place on the track. You also may walk up to check if the dog has stopped or indicated something on the track. Be careful not to do this too often, as you don't want the judges to get the impression that you are unsure of your dog's article indication.

If the puppy starts cutting the corners by more than ten feet, start putting a food drop within five to seven strides before the corner. Place the food drop after the turn closer to the corner as well. If your puppy is not even recognizing the turns, he needs a little remedial work before proceeding on. Repeat the first four days of turns, and then lay a two turn track. Use a shuffle step laid for the first few yards of the new leg at each turn. Do this for a couple of training sessions. If your puppy tracks that successfully, you may then proceed with single laid track as shown in the lesson charts.

Some dogs may have trouble finding the turn when the second leg is downwind because the wind is blowing the track scent away from him. Just work on that until he can handle that situation confidently. To help him understand this situation, use plenty of food drops on that downwind leg.

When working on turns, keep two goals in mind: Learn to read your dog, especially the pup's "I've lost the track" and "I've found the track" signs. And teach your puppy that the track doesn't go straight forever. Tracks do change direction.

LESS THAN PERFECT DAYS

A successful session of training is exhilarating, filled with joy for me, but it doesn't always teach you something new. Don't be discouraged by unsuccessful sessions. These less than perfect sessions will teach you the most interesting things and help you learn more about your dog, scent, weather, map making and all other aspects of tracking. If you are open and sensitive to what you and your dog experience as partners you will learn unexpected lessons. Both members of this team train each other. Dogs know more about scent and scenting than humans can ever hope to comprehend or measure. Be open to what your dog can teach you.

7

ADVANCED TRAINING

STRANGER LAID TRACKS

If you or just one other person has been consistently laying all your own tracks up until now, you will eventually need to have several other folks lay track for you and your puppy. He should not think that every track would have only your own scent or that of someone else who has laid tracks for you several times. When a brand new person lays track for you, you should look at the maps with the tracklayer before you run these tracks with your puppy. The tracklayer should follow behind as you run your puppy on the track. It's a good practice for your pup anyway as there will be two judges and a tracklayer following you in a test. Your puppy may as well get used to that. Once you have started the dog on the track, ask for the tracklayer's help only when absolutely necessary. Just a few stranger laid tracks will demonstrate to you that your puppy can and will track other people's scent.

BLIND TRACKS

Up until now, we have focused on tracks where you—the handler—knows in advance the layout of the track (or at least the general layout). Blind tracks—those where the handler does not know anything about the track except the location of the two start flags—represent a more difficult challenge. I am not a big fan of running lots of blind tracks with an inexperienced pup as it can frustrate both you and the dog. However, after your puppy has become a confident tracker, try one or two blind tracks. It is really thrilling for the handler to experience success on a blind track. It increases your confidence in your dog's ability and your confidence in your ability to read him. It is important for you and your dog to have at least some blind tracking experience if you plan to enter a tracking dog test because, of course, all tests are done on blind tracks. I recommend that you train on blind tracks that are laid by an experienced tracklayer. You should not even see the map before running the track. This track must be completely unknown to the handler. When doing a blind track in training, always carry an extra glove to throw down for the dog to find in case you need to end the track without completing it. You don't want the dog to become discouraged even if you do not do well with the blind track. Remember, never carry gloves during a tracking test.

When running a blind track, use the same line handling techniques you have used on known tracks or you will really confuse the pup. I realize it is difficult, but no matter how hard it is, you must try to handle the dog and line the same way whether you know the track or not. If you don't build up enough skill and confidence by training on blind tracks, then you might, like many handlers, put much more pressure on the dog in a tracking test than you ever did in training. It's helpful if the dog has felt that kind of pressure a time or two in training, but save that for the stage where you feel your puppy has the confidence to handle it without becoming de-motivated.

One way for a novice handler to avoid these problems is by running a blind track behind a good tracking dog. This can be a great confidence builder for the handler. If you know anyone who will allow you to handle the line behind a finished tracking dog on a blind track, go for it. It will be an exciting learning experience for you. You will be surprised at how this affects your handling. We all tend to make a dog really prove himself when we don't know where the track is. We don't think we handle differently, but we do. When tracking with an experienced dog, you will, quite naturally, trust the dog. This is how you want to behave in a test—let the dog do the work!

If you are having difficulty reading the pup on blind and stranger laid tracks, invite one or two people to watch you and your puppy on the track. It may be helpful to station these observers where they can see the dog from the side, front, or other angles as he approaches a turn. Remember to place them far enough away from the track that their scent does not confuse the dog. You might have them use binoculars. Ask for precise and specific observations of your dog's loss of track indicators and what your puppy does when he finds the scent again. It could be as simple as the observer noticing that when the dog reacquires the track scent his wagging tail hits the tracking line. This is something you might not notice while handling the dog.

COMPLEX TRACKS

If your puppy can do one turn and handle crosswinds, he can do two turns. If he can do two turns he can do three turns. He has already tracked several hundred yards in a single session. Now we simply use that distance on one track with several turns. You may now track a single track for each lesson and work/practice only three or four days a week.

TRAINING TIPS FOR COMPLEX TRACKS

- Vary the time of day that you track. Make sure you lay some tracks with "dry shoes." This means you laid the track in completely dry vegetation.
- Lay tracks on hills and in small gullies. These dips in the land are usually animal runs and are filled with distracting scents. Use an extra food drop or two beyond the gully or hilltop.
- Lay tracks across minor changes of vegetation, car tracks, and then perhaps across a gravel or paved drive. I prefer to be over prepared rather than the opposite.
- Stick to the schedule on increasing the age of the tracks (see Chapter 6) unless your puppy shows you he has a problem. Remember in hot, dry or windy weather the apparent age of the track to the pup will be older than the actual age of the track. If he has a problem, use extra food drops and skillful line handling to help your puppy learn how to handle that specific tracking situation.

- Keep quiet! My feeling is the less you verbalize to the dog, the better he'll do solving a problem. You don't want him looking to you or taking his focus away from the track.
- Track your pup in all kinds of weather. The only things that will stop a test are thunder and lightning. Sometimes an extreme downpour or snowstorm may delay a test, but the judge's definition may be different from yours. Over prepare.
- Once you have tracked the pup on a track that is two hours old, vary the age of training tracks from 30 minutes to two hours. Don't do too many two hour tracks. Tracks in a test are usually within the 30 minute to one hour range. Dogs that have done lots of work on two hour old tracks often have difficulty with tracks 30 minutes old. It almost seems like there is too much scent for them.
- Be sure not to over-feed your puppy on non-tracking days to help maintain his motivation on tracking days.
- Occasionally leave a wallet, shoe, hat or sock as a track article. Sometimes drop a glove in the middle of a track. Extra gloves are sometimes encountered in test tracks. By now he should also be picking up that glove and turning to you or even taking a few steps toward you. Make sure your puppy will track on after he finds that first glove. Take the glove from your puppy, praise him and ask him to go on tracking.

Don't overtax the puppy as you take on more complex tracks. If he has a problem, try to figure out what the real difficulty is. Make sure that the problem area is the only challenge he encounters while training to overcome the problem. If article indication is a problem, lay lots of straight, easy, article laden tracks, until you see that your puppy is showing he can handle the problem well. If he's having a problem tracking into the wind, go back to the crosswind tracks for a few days and don't be concerned with anything else.

IT'S ALL IN YOUR DIARY

Since I can't personally instruct you or your dog, keeping a tracking diary is vital to solving any problems your puppy may have as you tackle more complex tracks. How else can you figure out what his problem is, if you don't make good notes on his progress? Note everything about the track and the dog's performance. Specifically where did you track? What was the terrain? What kind of track did you lay? How old was the track? What was the weather, wind, humidity, etc? What did the dog do? Then…why did he do that? The answers to these and other questions are nearly always in the diary. Let your diary be your guide. Once you understand what the problem is, make a plan to solve it. Be sure to only present one problem at a time to your puppy.

When my students encounter problems, I say, "Let's look at your diary." We try to find out what the real problem is. "Gosh, looks like your puppy usually has a hard time at the old mill field. What is different at the old mill field?" Or another example, "Your puppy seems to have difficulty tracking in the afternoon. Afternoon tracks may have consistently drier vegetation than morning or evening tracks. What else could be different in the afternoons? Maybe we need to lay some really simple afternoon tracks for a few days."

Tracking is the *best adventure* my dogs and I have enjoyed together. My tracking diaries are my most treasured souvenirs of all my work with dogs! What grand memories they contain of dogs that no longer grace my life.

8

CERTIFICATION AND AKC TRACKING TESTS

A certification track is a track laid by an AKC Tracking Judge and is essentially the same as a tracking test track. Being certified is a prerequisite to taking a tracking test. You must gain a certification before you can take the AKC Tracking Dog Test. Certification is a serious effort. Passing a certification track is a notable accomplishment for any dog and handler team. There is no lower or upper age limit on certification.

To prepare for certification, run the pup on a track that conforms to an AKC test track at least once or twice (see the Appendix for details on AKC regulations). In a test, the track will make between three and five turns, be 440-500 yards long and be 30 minutes to two hours old. I recommend you make your practice track 30-45 minutes old with three or four turns.

If you pass the certification test, you will receive a written statement from the tracking judge that includes wording to the effect that you are "ready to participate in an America Kennel Club licensed or member tracking test" along with date you passed and the judge's name and signature. A current certification statement, signed by the judge, must accompany any entry into an AKC Tracking Dog Test. The certifying judge's name will be listed in the test catalog along with your dog's name and your name. You must pass a certification test again if you go on to fail four successive AKC tracking tests. If you do not pass the certification test, ask the judge to review with you where you had problems and focus on making improvements in your training sessions before trying again.

ENTERING A TRACKING TEST

Most tracking events are listed in the AKC Gazette Events Calendar, but not all are. Check with a tracking judge or an experienced tracking person if possible. They will be aware of events in your area and can give you contacts for test giving clubs. A tracking test entry uses the same form as an obedience trial entry. Write "TD Test" in the space for obedience class entry.

It is prudent to enter several tests. You don't know if you will draw into a test or be assigned a position on the alternate list. Frequently the entries in a Tracking Dog test exceed the number of test tracks being offered. When this happens there is a drawing to see which entries are accepted to run in that test. The time and place of the drawing is stated in the test premium list. This is so that any interested parties may attend the draw if they wish. Those entries not drawn for a track in the test will be assigned a position on an alternate list. You will be informed by letter if you have drawn into a test, or, if not, what your position is on the alternate list. If the test is at a convenient location and you are number one on the alternate list, you may decide to attend the test. If you do draw into a test and pass, call the other test secretaries and cancel any other entries you have made as soon as possible. That will allow them to have an alternate take your place. If you are on an alternate list in other tests, but decide not to attend, it is good form to contact that test secretary. If there is any other reason that you would not be able to attend a test you have entered, contact the secretary right away to let her/him know you are not coming. Clubs almost always lose money on tracking events and it's heartbreaking for all concerned to see an available slot in a test go unfilled.

TIPS FOR THE BIG DAY

Tracking is one of the few fields of dog training where the title hangs in balance on a single day with a single effort. This is true for TD and TDX (Tracking Dog Excellent) and VST (Variable Surface Tracking) tests. It can be one of the best highs you will ever experience. Therefore you want to make every effort to give yourself the best possible chance to pass each test you enter.

When packing for a test, take all your tracking gear, including an extra tracking line. If you have to travel out of town, take a wind-up or battery operated alarm clock. Don't count on a motel wake up service or an electric alarm clock to get you to the test on time. The time for the drawing for tracks will be stated in your entry confirmation. If you are late and an alternate is present at the drawing, your place in the test may be given to the alternate.

It is wise to locate the tracking field the night before the test and find out what the approximate travel time is between your motel and the tracking grounds. You will see flags in the fields. *Ignore those flags!* The surest way to fail in a test is to think you already know where the track goes. The dog knows! You have trained him well. You will increase your chance to fail if you try to anticipate the layout of the track. There is no way to discern the shape of a track by looking at or even memorizing the position of some flags in a field. You will also cheat yourself of one of the greatest thrills in dog training, that being following a track you cannot see! Don't track your puppy the day before a test. Although he might track well, you run the risk that you or your puppy might lose confidence in each other if your practice session is not a success.

Several tracks are laid for a test and each is numbered. In the confirmation of your entry, you will see a stated time and place of the drawing for tracks on the morning of the test. A lottery system determines when and on what track you and your dog will run in the test. You must be present for this drawing that is almost always held near the test site. If you are not present, the test secretary may offer your spot to an alternate if one is present. If no alternate is present, the test secretary may opt to draw for you or may simply mark you absent.

TAKING THE TEST

At the test, spend some quiet time alone, away from other people and from your dog. Don't watch the dog that runs before yours, instead check your gear. Make sure all is in order. Don't listen to "war stories" until after you run your dog. War stories are seldom positive. Think about the great times you and your puppy have already had tracking. Think of success, visualizing him snatching up that glove and bringing it to you. When they call you, get your puppy out and give him a chance to eliminate before going to your tracking field.

Never hurry to the start flag. A few calming breaths will help you clear your mind. Let your puppy sniff the local vegetation for a few moments and get it sorted out before you take him to the start flag. Make sure your line is untangled before you attach it to the harness. Give the line a light tug before you attach it to the dog's harness to ensure that it is not snagged on anything. Take your time. These few calming moments may make a huge difference for both you and your puppy.

Start your puppy exactly as you have done in training. Reach down and tickle the vegetation and wait till he leans forward with his nose on the track. Stand up and wait until you feel that twenty foot knot before you step off from the first flag. You may ask the judges for permission to restart your dog if he has not passed the second flag. Usually a restart is a *last* resort. If the dog is working, don't interfere with him. He may still be sorting the local scents out. Be still and give him a chance.

Watch your dog as he shows you each new leg of the track. Watch for loss of track indications and watch your puppy indicate when he finds the track again. As the pup takes each new leg, choose a landmark that you believe he is headed for. It may not be the judge's landmark, but it will likely be close. Don't just focus on the landmark, but note it mentally, then watch your dog every step of the way. An occasional quick glance at the landmark you chose may reassure you, but remember you may not have chosen the right landmark. Above all, watch your dog.

Remember how many miles you've walked behind this dog. Trust him. Believe in him. He's doing something that is very natural to him. Don't make him work really hard to prove every leg and every turn to you. When you feel those end knots in your left hand, make a decision. Is he tracking or isn't he? Don't make your puppy drag you off of every corner. Don't be in a hurry to back up. That should be absolutely the last thing you try if you feel you and your puppy are lost. While it is true that a fast moving dog may overrun a corner, I've seen many handlers in tests back themselves and their dogs hopelessly off the track.

A tracking test in progress.

By the time the dog has completed three turns and is on the fourth leg, if he stops and indicates something, go up and look, it may be a critter hole but it might be the article. If it's not the article, go back to where you were and wait for him to track on again. You are allowed speak to the dog on the track. However, the only reason to do so is to encourage him to start again if he has quit. You are never allowed, by any kind of gesture or other body language, to indicate a direction in which you want him to search. To do so should cause the judge to fail the team. Let your puppy work things out unless he needs a mild, pleasant, verbal reminder to get back to business.

Read the section on "guiding the dog" in the regulations. It is not unusual for a track or parts of a track to actually be visible. In those situations the judges will be extremely vigilant about handlers guiding the dog. If a handler is observed guiding the dog the result will be the dreaded whistle, indicating failure.

PASSING OR FAILING A TEST: SPORTSMANSHIP AND GOOD MANNERS

Passing a tracking test is beyond wonderful. Everyone there knows the time and miles you have put in with your puppy. Cheers and even a few tears are completely acceptable and appropriate. Be sure to get photos. The test-giving organization is required to provide an event catalog at the test site. This will include judges and all the information on your dog and the other dog and handler teams in the test. These are important mementos, be sure to take one home. Somehow a special bonding occurs between folks who pass at the same test. You may want to correspond in the future. Recognize however that on Monday morning your Aunt Tillie may not understand how or what a wonderful thing it is that you and your puppy have accomplished. It doesn't make you famous and you don't earn any valuable monetary reward. If you are lucky, Aunt Tillie might know that you really care about this and she's happy for you. But it is only your fellow trackers who can comprehend the heart pounding joy that you are feeling, especially if it's your first tracking title.

Not passing a tracking test is tough. It will mean going back, working some more, learning some more, spending some more money on entry fees and travel, and trying again. If, after the whistle blows, meaning the team has failed the test, you are offered the opportunity to complete the track with the tracklayer, by all means take it. It's a great chance to learn more about the terrain and your dog.

Whether or not you and your dog pass, never criticize or critique anyone else at the test, even if asked to do so. Don't listen to anyone else who may be griping about something regarding the test. Don't criticize or critique the judging, the club, the tracks, the tracklayers and certainly not your fellow participants, their dogs, handling techniques, or style of equipment. Every judge, club member and test committee member has worked very hard for no monetary reward to give you and your dog a chance to be tested. If you really feel you have a legitimate gripe, keep your mouth shut and write to the AKC and let them deal with it. At the event, at that moment, as one of my mentors used to say, "You pays your money…you takes your best shot…you acts like ladies and gents."

Don't solicit advice from other trackers or judges on what you or your dog did wrong in training. That's not fair to them, as they can't possibly know all that you and your puppy have done in training. Really experienced trackers usually don't offer unsolicited advice. So, if unsolicited advice is offered to you, take it with a very large grain of salt.

Most clubs provide a complimentary lunch. If your time will allow, stay for lunch. If you did not pass, don't feel embarrassed. Don't make excuses, just share in the joy of the group. Everyone there knows how much effort you have made just to get ready and get into a test. They'll all be hoping that you do better next time.

Here is an invitation for readers. Please feel free to share your tracking stories with me. You may contact me through my web site www.firedogenterprises.com. I always enjoy hearing your tales of the tracking trials or tribulations or triumphs.

9

WORKING WITH ADULT DOGS

My methods will work with a well-motivated adult dog. By this I mean a hungry dog. All my tracking students with adult dogs are told to give their dog his one meal only on the track at the last article. This is to be the only food the dog gets other than treats used in training. This is no real hardship on a healthy *adult* dog. If the dog is not well motivated to track during the first two weeks of work, give him only half his normal meal, again only at the last glove of the training session. If he then becomes motivated to track, he goes back to the normal amount of food, which he gets only on the tracking field. In calculating the amount of food the dog gets, be sure to count the food used as food drops in the total amount.

Remember too, that food drops must be something smelly that the dog LOVES—a high-powered treat. These are often higher in calories than regular dog food. Many people use slices of turkey hot dogs. The food drops should be soft not crunchy. We don't want the dog spending too much time cleaning up crumbs. He should gobble the food drop right down and carry on tracking.

If an adult dog continues to lack motivation after the first two weeks of work, he may go home with no dinner. My attitude to the dog is then, "Gee, I'm sorry you don't want to do this today, maybe you will want to tomorrow!" In a multiple dog household, you may need to put the tracking dog outside or have someone take him for a walk while the others are fed so he won't feel too sorry for himself. The longest I have ever had a dog hold out is four days. Wild dogs in nature feast and then go without catching prey for several days. I have had to do this with only two dogs in over 20 years. A couple of my students have been uncomfortable with this manipulation of a dog's food. They chose not to continue tracking. Sometimes personal goals must be adjusted. In both cases the dogs in training were show dogs and the owners did not wish them to lose weight. I respect that decision.

Once the dog understands the tracking game, he often skips some of the food drops to get to the big goodies at the glove. Don't worry about this, and keep on using the food according to the schedule in the book. The food drops reassure the dog even if he doesn't stop to eat them.

My lesson plans have been used successfully with adult dogs simply by increasing the length of the tracks in the lessons. A fifteen-yard track is a nice track for a puppy or a very small adult dog, but it is way too short a track to be meaningful to most adult dogs. You should move to tracks of fifty yards or more early on in training. All other elements of the lesson plan remain the same for the older pup or adult dog. If you need to repeat a lesson occasionally, don't worry. Sometimes it takes slightly longer for the older dog to fit all the pieces of the puzzle together.

Adult dogs, especially those that have already had extensive training in other areas, may take a little longer to understand that tracking requires them to take a leader role. These highly trained dogs may be so accustomed to looking to the trainer/handler for guidance and control that they have a hard time taking the lead in tracking. Instead of informing the handler, "It goes this way!" the highly trained dog may want to query, "Does it go this way, boss?" A little extra patience and time are usually all that is needed. The dog must have the confidence to tell the handler, "Yes! Here it is! I have found the track!" Puppies usually have no confidence problems.

Pay careful attention to reaching the goals stated in the lesson plans but don't worry if it takes a little longer to get the dog doing three or more turns. Often the hardest thing in training is to be still and wait for the mature dog to figure things out. As a former obedience competitor myself, I understand how difficult it can be for an accomplished trainer with a highly trained dog to back off and let the dog be the leader. Be patient with the adult tracking dog trainee.

Do not alter the schedule for increasing the age of tracks just because you are working with an adult dog. You may, however, back up on this aging of tracks schedule and work your way up to older tracks again if you believe the dog has an "age of track" problem.

This method can be used with senior dogs as well. Do you have any canine retirees that may be bored and feeling a little left out? Tracking is marvelous for these veterans. If your senior dog can walk and sniff and he likes to eat, give it a try. He will perk up with a new sense of pride and purpose. He's getting quality time with his best human buddy whether he ever earns a title or not. And of course that applies to any age dog you take the time to train to track!

APPENDIX

GENERAL REQUIREMENTS FOR AKC TRACKING DOG TESTS

Please note that I have summarized only those sections from the AKC Tracking Regulations handbook that I believe are particularly relevant or of interest to beginning trackers. You will want to become familiar with the entire handbook.

Tests may only be entered with dogs with an AKC registration or an ILP (Indefinite Listing Privilege) number. Dogs that are spayed or neutered may enter and bitches in season may compete if okayed by the tracking event secretary and by running the last track. Each entry for a non-tracking titled dog must also include a statement of certification from an AKC tracking test judge. This certification must state that the judge has observed the dog to successfully complete a track that is the equivalent of an official AKC tracking test. Dogs that have already earned at "TD" title may enter a tracking test for the fun of it but will be added to the drawing to get in only if not enough untitled dogs are entered. Untitled dogs are always given preference in the lottery to get into the test.

EQUIPMENT ALLOWED

- The dog must wear a plain harness when tracking.
- An inconspicuous marking is permitted on the harness to identify the dog in case of loss.
- If a collar is worn by the dog while tracking, the collar must meet the requirements of Chapter 2, Section 17 (collars) of the *Obedience Regulations* except that in a tracking test, required license or rabies tags may be attached to the collar.
- The leash shall be 20 to 40 feet in length.
- The leash shall be attached to the harness when tracking.
- The handler may carry plain water or ice on the track and may offer it to the dog.

GENERAL REQUIREMENTS

- No food or other motivational items may be carried on the track.
- There is no time limit as long as the dog is actively working the track. A dog judged not to be working will not be given any minimum time and must be marked failed.
- The tracking test article will be a glove or wallet of an inconspicuous color.
- The dog must identify and the dog or the handler must retrieve the article.
- Guiding or aiding the dog, especially if the track is visible, is cause for failure.
- Obedience regulations that would apply at an AKC obedience trial also apply to tracking events. For example there will be no training of any kind on the grounds for the duration of the tracking event.
- No dog may be entered in a TDX or VST test until after earning a TD Title.

TRACKING DOG TEST TRACK REQUIREMENTS

- The track shall be at least 440 yards long and not more that 500 yards in length.
- There will be two flags on the first leg of the track, one at the start and the second 30 yards past the start. The judges shall indicate which of the two flags is the start flag in the case of a restart. The two flag start indicates the direction of the first leg of the track.
- The length of each of the legs of the track shall be at least 50 yards, except the first turn must be 30 yards beyond the second flag.
- The scent on the track shall be not less than thirty (30) minutes or more than two (2) hours old.
- A total of three (3) to five (5) turns shall be used. Both left and right 90-degree angle turns shall be used. No acute angle turns are to be used. The first turn must be more that thirty (30) yards from the second flag.

- At least two (2) of the turns shall be right angle (90 degree) turns and there should be more that two (2) such turns.
- At least two (2) of the right angle turns shall be well out in the open, where there are no fences or boundaries to guide the dog.
- No part of the track shall follow any fence or boundary within 15 yards of such fence or boundary.
- No part of the track may be within 50 yards of any other part of the same track.
- Consecutive parallel tracks shall not be used.
- No part of any track may be laid within 75 yards of another track. However, with two tracks going in opposite directions from the same areas, the starting flags may be as close as 50 yards to each other.
- A track shall not cross a body of water or a paved road.
- No TD track should have changes of cover that would be suit able for a TDX obstacle.
- No conflicting (cross) tracks shall be used.
- In a TD test the article shall be a glove or wallet of an inconspicuous color.

TRACKING DOG EXCELLENT TEST REQUIREMENTS
- Your dog has passed the TD test.
- There shall be a single flag start so not to indicate the direction of the first leg.
- The track shall be at least 800 yards and not more than 1000 yards in length.
- The length of each leg shall be at least 50 yards.
- The track shall be at least 3 hours but not more that 5 hours old.
- A total of 5 to 7 turns shall be used.
- The first turn shall be in an open area.
- Acute angles should never be used except in unusual circumstances of terrain.
- At least 3 and preferably more than 3 turns shall be right angle turns.

- No part of the track shall be within 50 yards of any other part of the track or within 75 yards of any other track.
- Two sets of cross tracks shall be laid at least 1 hour and 30 minutes after the laying of the main track, and these two sets shall cross the main track in two widely separated places.
- Cross tracks shall not be within 30 yards of an article or an obstacle or within 50 yards of a turn nor within 75 yards of the start of the track.
- The track shall cross at least two obstacles such as gullies, plowed ground, streams, fences or lightly traveled roads.
- There shall be no obstacles on the first leg.
- There shall be 4 articles, one of which is left at the start flag and the fourth, which is left at the end of the track. The remaining 2 articles shall be left at widely spaced intervals on the track.
- Articles shall be 4 dissimilar personal articles about the same size as a wallet or glove.
- Articles shall be dropped more that 30 yards from any turn, obstacle or cross track.

Keep in mind the regulations may change. The pamphlets that are available from AKC which outline the regulations for the TD and the Guidelines for Tracking Test judges are required reading for you if you want to pass the test. How silly to fail because you haven't studied the rules. The most current rules and regulations for tracking will always be available for downloading on the American Kennel Club web site, http://www.akc.org or email orderdesk@akc.org.

Single copies are free; there is a small charge for additional copies. You can also order via mail from:

American Kennel Club Order Desk
5580 Centerview Drive
Raleigh, NC 27606-3390
Phone: 919.233.9767
Fax: 919.816.3627

RECOMMENDED READING

Tracking Regulations. American Kennel Club

Obedience Regulations. American Kennel Club

*Tracking Dog-Theory and Method. Glen Johnson

*Mastering Variable Surface Tracking. Ed Presnall

*Fun Nosework for Dogs. Roy Hunter

Go Find! Training Your Dog to Track. L. Wilson Davis (out of print)

*Scent.   Milo Pearsall & Hugo Verbruggen

Hunting by Scent. H.M. Budgett (out of print)

*Following Ghosts. John Rice and Suzanne Clothier

*Tracking From the Ground Up. Sandy Ganz and Susan Boyd

*These and hundreds of other excellent books on dogs are available from www.dogwise.com.

AUTHOR BIOGRAPHY

Carolyn Krause is the training and behavior consultant to the Bradford Park Veterinary Hospital and Grant Avenue Pet Hospital group. She has instructed classes in obedience training and tracking dog training for many years for the Springfield Dog Training Club. She was the original Director of Training at Happy Tails Doggie Day Care and Training Center in Springfield, Missouri. Carolyn is the developer and director of the Positively Puppies program of classes that are given at several veterinary clinics. She's a professional level member of the Association of Pet Dog Trainers.

Carolyn has been tracking for many years and has given tracking dog training seminars in several states. Two of her Dalmatians, Becky the Fire Dog, (UDTX, TDI, Delta Dog Pet Partner 0006) and Poppy the Fire Dog, (CH, CDX, TD, TDI, CPC, Delta Dog Pet Partner 0011) served over 15 years as the fire safety education mascots of the Springfield Missouri Fire Department. She has also been involved in obedience competition, tracking dog training and animal-assisted therapy programs. Her dogs and her students' dogs have worked in both still and video modeling. Carolyn is an emeritus American Kennel Club Tracking Test Judge.

Carolyn is an award-winning writer, whose work has appeared in several national and regional dog-related publications.